FAMOUS PRESIDENTIAL SCANDALS

DON LAWSON

ENSLOW PUBLISHERS, INC.

Bloy St. & Ramsey Ave.
Box 777
Hillside, N.J. 07205
U.S.A.

P.O. Box 38
Aldershot
Hants GU12 6BP
U.K.

Gift 10/02 973.0992 $20.00

Library of Congress Cataloging-in-Publication Data

Lawson, Don.
  Famous presidential scandals / Don Lawson.
  p. cm.
  Includes bibliographical references.
  ISBN 0-89490-247-4
  1. Presidents—United States—History. 2. Corruption (in politics)—United
States—History. 3. United States—Politics and government—1865-1900. 4. United
States—Politics and government—20th century. I. Title.

E176.1.L3 1990
973'.0992—dc20   89-35874
                                                                      CIP

Printed in the United States of America

10 9 8 7 6 5 4 3 2 1

Illustrations Courtesy of the Library of Congress

Contents

Preface 5

Section One
*The Grant Administration's Crédit Mobilier and
Whiskey Ring Scandals*

1 Ulysses S. Grant: From Soldier to President 15

2 The Grant Administration 23

Section Two
The Harding Administration's Teapot Dome Scandal

3 Warren G. Harding: From Country Editor to President . . 39

4 The Harding Administration 49

Section Three
The Nixon Administration's Watergate Scandal

5 Richard M. Nixon: From Young Lawyer
     to President 63

6 The Nixon Administration 75

Section Four
The Reagan Administration's Iran-Contra Scandal

7 Ronald W. Reagan: From Sports Broadcaster and
     Actor to President 95

8 The Reagan Administration 105

Further Reading 123
Index 125

Preface

Historians are generally agreed that it is remarkable that so few scandals have occurred during the administrations of the more than forty U.S. presidents. Historians and political observers also agree that it is even more remarkable that what few scandals there have been have only rarely involved the president himself.

Only one president has been impeached by the U.S. House of Representatives. He was the first post-Civil War president, Andrew Johnson, who got into a violent dispute with Congress regarding the president's legal power over the defeated South. Although this dispute led to Johnson's impeachment, he was acquitted in the impeachment trial before the Senate. Interestingly, Johnson, who had been a U.S. senator several years before becoming vice president under Abraham Lincoln, returned to the Senate in 1875, half a dozen years after he left office as president.

A part of Johnson's dispute with Congress unfortunately involved Ulysses S. Grant, the general in command of all of the Union armies during the Civil War. This involvement was much against Grant's wishes and led to such bitter feelings between the two men that the outgoing President Johnson refused to attend the inauguration ceremonies in which Grant succeeded him.

The difficulties between Johnson and Grant grew out of Johnson's efforts to carry out what he believed would have been Lincoln's generous policies of reconstruction and reconciliation with the South. Lincoln had been assassinated on Good Friday, April 14, 1865. There were a number of members of Congress, both representatives and senators, who disagreed with Johnson's proposed humanitarian treatment of the defeated South. Secretary of War Edwin M. Stanton agreed with these dissidents and publicly said so. Mainly to prevent Johnson from moving against Stanton, Congress passed the so-called Tenure of Office Act in March of 1867, which prevented any president from removing a cabinet officer without Senate approval.

In open defiance of this act, President Johnson dismissed Secretary of War Stanton and replaced him with a reluctant General Grant. The Senate, of course, immediately declared Johnson's action illegal and in January of 1868 reinstated Stanton. Grant thereupon returned to his army duties, and Stanton resumed his role as head of the War Department. It was Grant's hasty departure from the War Department and his ready return to active duty that created the breach between him and Johnson. Johnson wrote Grant criticizing him for not even consulting with him, the president, before making his move and accusing Grant of failing to live up to his word.

This infuriated Grant, who wrote Johnson that Congress was, after all, the final authority and that to go against this authority would be in violation of the law. The two men never spoke again.

Meanwhile, in February of 1868 President Johnson again replaced Stanton, this time with a temporary general, Lorenzo Thomas. Late in that same month the House of Representatives passed the following resolution: "Resolved that Andrew Johnson be impeached of high crimes and misdemeanors." Specific charges included "usurpation of the law, corrupt use of the veto power, interference at elections, and misdemeanors."

The actual impeachment proceedings took place in the Senate between March 13 and May 26, 1868. Chief Justice of the United States Salmon P. Chase presided. There were then just fifty-four members of the Senate, and a two-thirds vote was required for conviction. When the final vote took place in late May, thirty-five senators voted for conviction and nineteen for acquittal. Johnson thus escaped conviction and removal from office by one lone vote. The Tenure of Office Act was finally repealed in 1887.

Grant's troubles with presidential cabinets and the Congress of the United States did not end with his brief skirmish during the Johnson administration. His own administration, unfortunately, became sullied with greed, graft, and corruption during what was known as the Crédit Mobilier stock scandal. Some of his aides were also involved in the scandal-ridden "Whiskey Ring," and less than two years before his death a New York banking firm in which one of Grant's sons was a partner failed, leaving the general and his wife and family penniless. These trying events are related in detail in Section One of this volume.

Warren G. Harding was never threatened with impeachment. He was, in fact, one of the nation's most popular presidents. There are those, however, who think that Harding might have been impeached if he had lived long enough to face a Senate investigation of illicit government oil leases involving Harding's secretary of the interior, Albert B. Fall. This blossomed into the notorious Teapot Dome scandal, which resulted in Fall's being sent to jail—the first cabinet member to be convicted of a crime. Teapot Dome and other scandals involving the Harding administration as well as Harding's somewhat mysterious and premature death are told about in Section Two.

President Richard M. Nixon probably avoided being impeached by resigning as president—the first U.S. chief executive to do so. Nixon was one of the rare presidents who did seem to be involved in the scandal that brought down their own administrations.

Known as the Watergate scandal or Watergate affair, the Nixon misdeeds started with a break-in at the Democratic National Committee's headquarters at the Watergate apartment-office complex in Washington, D.C. The Watergate burglars were all henchmen of incumbent Republican President Nixon bent on robbing the Democratic political files and planting telephone "bugs" and wiretaps to gain political information. The burglars were caught in the act.

Immediately after the apprehension of the Watergate burglars, there was no connection made between them and the president of the United States. Eventually, however, Nixon and some twenty-four of his aides were disclosed as having taken part in either the planning, carrying out, or cover-up of the Watergate affair. The details of Watergate, the disclosure of incriminating tape recordings of conversations made by Nixon in the Oval Office, the threats by Congress of impeachment, Nixon's resignation, and his pardon by President Gerald R. Ford are related in Section Three.

Ronald W. Reagan was an extremely popular president. Because no criticism of Reagan seemed to stick to him and because misdeeds by his aides seemed to slide off him, Reagan was often called the "Teflon" president. (Teflon is the stick-proof, slippery chemical coating applied to such cooking utensils as frying pans). Nevertheless, during Regan's second term in office, events occurred that threatened to destroy his fault-free reputation if not his whole administration. These events became known as the Iran-Contra affair.

This affair included secret and perhaps illegal involvement with countries in the Middle East and Central America by several American government officials and Reagan aides. Terrorists in the Middle East had seized a number of U.S.citizens and held them hostage for many months. In an effort to free these hostages, some of Reagan's aides decided to make secret deals to offer military arms and supplies to these terrorists in Iran. In exchange, the United States would gain not only their freedom but also monetary payment for some of the military material. Money from these sales would then be secretly siphoned off to the revolutionary Reagan-backed Contra cause in Nicaragua. The Contras were trying to overthrow the Nicaraguan Sandinista government that the Reagan administration opposed because it believed the Sandinistas were Communist oriented and supported by the Soviet Union.

Much of this secret activity by the American officials was of a highly questionable legal nature. But the real issue was how directly the president himself was involved in the Iran-Contra affair. The answers are given in Section Four of this book.

Today, we have greatly expanded means of compiling information. Modern administrations, like the Reagan administration, are subject to intense scrutiny. Wrongdoing, or at least suspected wrongdoing, is exposed by the media in ways that were never possible years ago.

The author would like to point out that after each scandal during a presidential administration, it has become almost fashionable for the public to make sarcastic and even vicious comments about the integrity of our elected officials in particular and politicians in general. Such a practice is truly unfortunate because, among other things, it discourages young people from following careers in government and public service. And without the constant infusion of bright young minds into our government, this country cannot remain the strong and influential model of democracy that it has been from its very beginning. Broad, unwarranted accusations about government officials are also unjust because the honest officeholders by far outnumber the dishonest ones.

But why then a book about presidential scandals? Because there have been so relatively few, they rouse interest. Further, a disclosure of just where and why some of our elected and appointed government officials have gone wrong may help future administrations avoid these or similar pitfalls.

—D.L.

Section One

The Grant Administration's Crédit Mobilier and Whiskey Ring Scandals

Ulysses S. Grant

1

Ulysses S. Grant:
From Soldier to President

A strangely contradictory man, quiet, mild-mannered Ulysses S. Grant was in many ways a military genius and a civilian incompetent. Although he served two terms in office as the nation's eighteenth president between 1869 and 1877, Grant is today remembered more as a successful general of the Union army in the Civil War than he is as a chief executive of the United States. In fact, if his two terms in office are remembered at all, they are usually associated with scandals.

Ulysses Simpson Grant was born near Cincinnati, Ohio, on April 27, 1822. He was the oldest of six children, three boys and three girls, born to Jesse Root Grant and Hannah Simpson Grant. Ulysses' given first name was actually Hiram, but due to a mistake by the congressman who appointed him to West Point, the Hiram was dropped and Ulysses' mother's maiden family name was added. Thus the young cadet became Ulysses Simpson or U. S. Grant. This slip-up pleased young Grant, who preferred being called either "Uncle Sam" or just "Sam" by his classmates rather than by his actual initials HUG.

Sam Grant had obtained his West Point appointment through the efforts of his father, who was successful in the leather tanning business and active in local politics. Young Grant regarded the West Point appointment merely as a means of getting a college education. He did not especially like the military and had no plans to follow a military career. However, immediately after graduating and receiving his commission as a second lieutenant, Grant was assigned to Jefferson Barracks, Missouri. There he met Julia Dent, and within three months the couple were engaged. But the wedding was delayed by the beginning of the war with Mexico.

Grant had an outstanding combat record in the Mexican War, fighting in almost every battle. He returned from the war a brevet or temporary captain, and he and Julia were married in August of 1848. Now the paradox of Grant showed itself for the first time. He simply was not a good peacetime soldier. Mentioned frequently in dispatches for bravery during the Mexican War, efficiency reports on Grant during peacetime reflected a slovenly dressed soldier who drank too much.

Nevertheless, Grant continued to serve in the army for several years, first at Sackett's Harbor, New York, then at Detroit, Michigan, and finally on the Pacific Coast. During this period the Grants' first two children were born, Frederick Dent in 1850 and Ulysses, Jr., in 1852. Two more children, Ellen or "Nellie" and Jesse Root, would be born in 1855 and 1858 respectively.

Despite his growing family responsibilities, Grant failed to apply himself as an army officer. Finally the colonel in charge of his company requested Grant's resignation, which was the same thing as getting fired from a civilian job. Out of work and out of funds, Grant had to borrow money to get to Missouri, where Julia's father had bought the Grants a small farm.

But Grant was no peacetime farmer either. Soon "Hardscrabble," as Grant nicknamed the farm, failed. The impoverished ex-army officer and ex-son-of-the-soil then took to selling real estate in and around St. Louis, but he barely made enough money on commissions to feed his family.

By this time Grant's father, Jesse, had moved from Ohio to Illinois, where he had established a successful leather business at Galena. Grant was offered a job there, and he and his family had little choice but to move to Galena. Almost forty years old, Ulysses S. Grant was a clerk in a leather goods store and generally regarded as a failure when the Civil War broke out.

But the North soon found it needed every man with any military training that it could muster, and Grant was put in charge of a regiment of volunteers from Galena and the surrounding territory. Within a few weeks Illinois Governor Richard Yates made Grant a colonel in charge of these volunteers. The appointment and familiar military responsibility worked wonders on Grant. A friend and neighbor later said: "I saw new energies in him. He dropped a stoop-shouldered way of walking and set his hat forward on his forehead in a jaunty fashion."

Grant himself admitted: "I never went into our leather store again, to put up a package or to do any other business."

Before long Grant—now a brigadier general—established his headquarters at Cairo, Illinois, and moved his men there to prepare for combat. The first actions in which they engaged were minor skirmishes in Missouri. But as soon as the guns began to sound even in these small encounters, Grant's men noted an even greater change in him. Vague and irresolute as a peacetime civilian, Grant became decisive and sure of himself once in battle. To his men he always seemed fearless under fire. This Grant insisted was simply not so. He just didn't show any fear. The enemy, he said, was just as much afraid as he was, which evened things up. Nevertheless, one of his soldiers, a private, summed up his men's feelings on the subject: "Ol' Ulys'," the soldier said, "just don't scare worth a damn."

Whatever the cause of his transformation, an authoritative, resolute Grant next successfully led his men into Paducah, Kentucky. They also attacked a Confederate camp at Belmont, Missouri, and then settled down for additional training to prepare for what Grant accurately foresaw as a long, hard war. Grant now had some 20,000 men under his command.

Early in 1862 Grant successfully led campaigns against Fort Henry on the Tennessee River and Fort Donelson on the Cumberland

River. Fort Henry was captured with relative ease, but Donelson proved a tougher nut to crack. When it was about to fall after extremely bitter fighting, the Confederate commander, General Simon Buckner, sent a message to Grant asking him what terms he would accept for capitulation. Despite the fact that before the war Buckner and Grant had been close friends—it was Buckner who had loaned Grant the money that enabled him to return from California—Grant's unequivocal reply came back loud and clear: "No terms except an unconditional and immediate surrender can be accepted. I propose to move immediately upon your works." From that point on, the initials U. S. in Grant's name came to stand for "Unconditional Surrender."

Grant had been greatly aided in the capture of Fort Donelson by Commodore A. H. Foote and his fleet of gunboats, but it was Grant who emerged in the nation's press as a Northern hero. Among other things it was the first important victory of the war for the North, and some 15,000 Confederates had been taken prisoner—the greatest number of prisoners in American military history up to that time.

From this point forward, General U. S. Grant went on to victory after victory in the western theater of war. Not all of these battles were easily won—Shiloh was a particularly bitter and bloody affair—and if there was one solid criticism that could be leveled against Grant, it was that he never hesitated to continue to commit his men to battle no matter how high the casualty tolls were. Nevertheless, after a severe setback the first day at Shiloh, and then at Vicksburg, the Confederacy's most powerful stronghold on the Mississippi River, he was successful. Interestingly, Grant's son Fred, who was just thirteen, served with his father during the Vicksburg campaign.

Other generals, jealous of Grant's meteoric rise, began to carry false tales of Grant's incompetence to Lincoln. The president's terse response was: "I can't spare this man—he fights." Then stories began to reach Lincoln about Grant's drinking. These tales too were untrue since Grant did not drink once he went into a combat situation. It was peacetime soldiering and peacetime civilian life that bored Grant to distraction and made him resort to the bottle. Nevertheless, the stories persisted, and finally Lincoln suggested to the tale-bearers that they find out what brand Grant drank so he could supply the same kind to the rest of the Northern generals.

Grant's reaction after the initial setback at Shiloh on April 6, 1862, gave insight into his determination to succeed as a military commander in the face of severe adversity. Grant's forces had been taken by surprise near Pittsburg Landing along the Tennessee River and had almost been driven back into the river by the Confederates under General A. S. Johnston. Complete collapse had been averted only by Grant's personal intervention at several key points, where he rallied his men to stand and fight. But after the first day of the Battle of Shiloh—named after a church which stood nearby—things looked dim indeed for the North.

That night General William T. Sherman, one of Grant's classmates at West Point and now one of his trusted aides, appeared at Grant's battlefield headquarters to see if Grant had in mind orders for a retreat the next day. Sherman himself had also been all over the battlefield that day, having at least one horse shot out from under him and narrowly escaping capture at another time.

He found Grant standing under a tree, only partially sheltered from a steady rain that had begun to fall. Grant was smoking a cigar that he managed to keep protected under the broad brim of his campaign hat.

Later, reporting the meeting in his own memoirs, Sherman said, "Some wise and sudden instinct" prompted him not to mention retreat to Grant. Instead he said, "Well, Grant, we've had the devil's own day, haven't we?"

Puffing on his cigar, Grant said, "Yes. Yes, we have." Then, after another puff: "Lick 'em tomorrow, though!"

And "lick 'em" he and his men did.

As a reward for the capture of Vicksburg, Grant was promoted to major general and placed in command of all of the Northern armies of the West. Soon he captured Chattanooga, Tennessee, by sending Union troops up the seemingly impassable heights of Lookout Mountain and Missionary Ridge, where Confederate troops protected the approaches to Chattanooga. Once these high points were successfully stormed, not only Chattanooga but also the whole of Tennessee was virtually in Union hands and the power of the Confederacy in the West was broken.

But so far as the Union was concerned, the war in the East had not been going so well. There, nobody seemed a match for the great Confederate Robert E. Lee. To remedy this situation, Lincoln summoned Grant to Washington, where he arrived in March of 1864. Lincoln immediately promoted Grant to lieutenant general and placed him in command of all the Union armies.

Personally taking command of the Northern army in the East on May 4, 1864, Grant prepared to attack Lee's army in northern Virginia in what amounted to a frontal assault. In an area known as the Wilderness near Chancellorsville, Grant was badly beaten. But unlike other Northern generals Lee had met, Grant did not beat a hasty retreat. Despite severe losses Grant stood his ground and then went back on the attack, stating flatly, "I propose to fight it out on this line if it takes all summer."

There followed some of the bloodiest fighting of the war. Eventually, however, Lee's sources of supply were cut off, and he was forced to abandon the Confederate capital at Richmond. Grant immediately occupied the city. When told by his aides that further fighting was futile, Lee said, "Then there is nothing left for me to do but go and see General Grant."

The two generals met at Appomattox Courthouse on Palm Sunday, April 9, 1865, for the surrender ceremony. Afterward scattered fighting continued for a short time, but the long war was over. Its aftereffects, however, were to linger for months and even years, and it was into this troubled political situation that Grant, the political innocent, soon moved.

Immediately after the war, of course, Grant was the hero of the hour in the North. But following the assassination of President Lincoln and Vice President Andrew Johnson's succession to the presidency, something approaching revolution seemed to threaten the nation. Johnson's problems with Congress, his eventual impeachment over Reconstruction, and his apparent inability to govern the war-torn country made people look to Grant as the savior in peacetime that he had been in war.

Actually Grant had never had any real interest in politics, and he had none now. But the honors heaped on him after the war made him want to repay the people in some way through public service. Not only had he been made a full general—a rank not used since George Washington's day—but hundreds of thousands of dollars in gifts had been given to him and his family. With the independent income they now had, Mrs. Grant would have been happy to retire with her family to the house in Galena that had also been given to the Grants by grateful citizens. But her husband felt duty-bound to at least consider running for the presidency.

While the Senate was engaged in President Johnson's impeachment trial, the Republicans held their convention in Chicago and on May 21, 1865, unanimously nominated Grant for president. Schuyler Colfax of Indiana was selected as Grant's vice presidential running mate. Campaigning under the slogan, "Let Us Have Peace," Grant handily defeated his Democratic opponent, Horatio Seymour, former governor of New York, 214 electoral votes to 80, although his popular vote majority was small, only slightly more than 300,000 votes out of about 5.5 million cast.

2

The Grant Administration

When forty-six-year-old Ulysses Grant moved into the White House on March 4, 1869, he was up to that time the youngest man to become president. Grant brought with him his wife and several children—his father Jesse also loved to visit there—but little or no experience in selecting administrative aides. Consequently, he made several irreparable early mistakes.

During the Civil War Grant had chosen old friends and acquaintances as his staff officers and aides. As a result, he did most of his own staff work. This was a workable arrangement for handling a large number of military combat units, each one of which was led by a competent commander who religiously followed Grant's orders. It was a totally unworkable way to govern a nation of millions of independent, free-spirited civilians.

In addition, in almost all of his Civil War battles Grant had personally covered the combat areas astride his own horse, Cincinnati. Grant was a superb horseman and easily outrode all of the members of his staff from the start of the war to its finish. Unfortunately, a nation could not be governed from horseback but required desk-bound supervision by the chief executive and a highly competent, honest staff of administrative aides—not incompetent and in come cases dishonest friends and cronies.

For his presidential cabinet Grant chose as secretary of war his former army chief of staff and old friend from Galena, John A. Rawlins, although Rawlins was mortally ill and Grant knew it. Rawlins died within a year. For secretary of state Grant chose Elihu Washburne, who soon resigned. His resignation was fortunate because his replacement, Hamilton Fish, proved to be quite able. Grant's first selection for secretary of the treasury, A. T. Stewart, was soon forced out of office because his business interests conflicted with his government job. George S. Boutwell replaced Stewart despite the fact that Boutwell came from Massachusetts and another Massachusetts man, E. R. Hoar, had already been named attorney general. In order to keep the voting public and the Congress in a cooperative mood, it is always wise for a president to make his appointments geographically widespread.

Another unpopular selection as far as many members of Congress were concerned was the appointment of a Seneca Indian, Ely S. Parker, as commissioner of Indian affairs. This selection, however, was typical of Grant's consistent attitude of fairness toward all Americans. Although he always said he had believed in the Northern cause in the Civil War because the South had to be kept in the Union, he was also an early opponent of slavery.

Soon after he took office as chief executive, the innocent and unsuspecting Grant discovered that corruption was widespread throughout the United States. Public morality seemed to be at an all-time low and was directly reflected in political morality. Part of this trend was due to the aftermath of the Civil War. Much of it, however, was due to the so-called "spoils system" that had become entrenched as a political part of life. Under this system politicians who were elected to office rewarded their supporters by giving them jobs in government whether or not they were qualified.

Although Grant had made his early appointments based on his own personal spoils system, he saw, to his credit, the dangers in its continued widespread use and tried to get the Congress to appropriate money to support a civil service or merit system for candidates for government jobs. But the Civil Service Act was not passed for several years, going into effect only in 1872.

Meanwhile, the hint of the first government scandal was not long in coming. In the late summer of 1869, with the Grants barely settled in the White House, a ring of financial speculators in New York City tried to gain control of or "corner" the gold market. Led by Jay Gould and James Fisk, Jr., these speculators figured that if they could corner the gold market, they could drive up the price of the precious metal and then sell their holdings at an enormous profit.

There was just one way this scheme could be stopped, and that was by the government dumping some of its own gold reserves on the open market. At this point President Grant's brother-in-law, Abel R. Corbin, contacted the gold speculators and told them that—for a price—he could prevail upon Grant not to allow the sale of any federal gold.

Corbin did not work for the government. Nevertheless, he assured the speculators that he was close enough to Grant to get him to do his bidding. But the scheme backfired when Grant was apparently informed of the deal and ordered his treasury secretary, George Boutwell, to put $4 million in gold on the market immediately. This effectively thwarted the scheme, although a brief financial panic could not be averted. The day on which the gold "corner" was destroyed was Friday, September 24, 1869. It became known as "Black Friday" and put the Grant administration in something of a shadow at its very outset.

For the most part, however, the rest of Grant's first term in office seemed to go along rather smoothly. But immediately beneath this calm surface, corruption had begun to boil and soon spilled over into the Grant administration.

The trouble had actually begun before Grant took office with the start of construction on America's first transcontinental railway. The railroad, which took four years to finish, was built westward from Omaha by the Union Pacific and eastward from Sacramento by the

Central Pacific. After four long years of difficult construction the two links were joined at a place called Promontory Point near Ogden, Utah, on May 10, 1869. At the ceremony opening the railway to transcontinental traffic the presidents of the Central Pacific and Union Pacific railroads, Leland Stanford and Thomas Durant, drove in golden spikes joining the two links. There was a national celebration on this auspicious day, and the men and women who had labored so long and faithfully to link the eastern and western United States were honored throughout the land.

But it was not long before the celebration began to turn sour as rumors spread of corruption at the highest levels of government during the railroad's construction and afterwards. The actual revelations of the alleged stock manipulations and payoffs to members of Congress as well as the vice president of the United States were not made until 1872, but before then it was fairly common knowledge what was happening.

The scandal revolved around a joint stock company used to finance the construction of the Union Pacific Railroad. The name of this company originally was the Pennsylvania Fiscal Agency, which had been founded in 1859. Near the end of the Civil War, with construction of the first transcontinental railroad well under way, the Union Pacific Company gained control of the Pennsylvania Fiscal Agency and turned it into a construction company for the Union Pacific. The agency's name was changed to Crédit Mobilier of America. Just why this name was chosen is not clear. There was a French banking firm known as Crédit Mobilier, and it may have been that the American promoters wanted to give their company an added air of distinction by adopting the fancy-sounding French name. They may also have been trying to attract foreign investors.

In any event, construction funds for the Union Pacific leg of the transcontinental railroad began to be funneled through this company. Authorized by the Congress, these construction funds were enormous. In fact, the men involved knew that there would be much more money to be made in building the railroad than there would be in operating it.

For each mile of track built, the U.S. govenrment gave the Union Pacific ten sections of public land bordering the railroad (a section was a piece of land one mile square), plus government bonds in amounts between $16,000 and $48,000, depending upon the difficulty of the country through which the railroad was being built. Needless to say, inspectors were encouraged to declare all land extremely difficult for railroad construction. (Encouragement in many cases meant bribes.)

The amount of money paid to the Union Pacific far exceeded the actual cost of construction. Nevertheless, the Union Pacific fed its fees to its construction company, Crédit Mobilier of America, and told its officers to make sure all of its construction fees were actually spent. Since the Union Pacific officers and the Crédit Mobilier officers were frequently the same people, such an arrangement was similar to a person taking money out of one pocket and putting it into another in the same pair of trousers. As a result of the enormous difference between what construction costs actually were and what the railroad officers were paid, the officers made huge profits. It was estimated, for example, that Oakes Ames, manager of Crédit Mobilier of America, and his brother Oliver made some $20 million.

Naturally word of these exorbitant profits soon began to reach the members of Congress, several of whom began to ask questions. To keep Congress quiet, Oakes Ames began to sell congressmen shares in the construction company at a price well below their market value. When some congressmen could not afford even these low prices, Ames loaned them the money at little or no interest to enable them to buy the stock, which paid dividends as high as 340 percent.

One of the reasons Oakes Ames had such a close relationship with Congress was because he himself was a congressman from Massachusetts. He and Oliver and another congressman, James Brooks of New York, worked together to keep the scheme in operation, but by no means were all of the congressmen, or even a majority of them, willing to go along with fleecing the government in this high-handed fashion.

Soon the story was leaked to the press, and in 1872 New York newspapers let the public in on the scandal. Congress immediately began an investigation, which finally resulted in severe reprimands being given to Oakes Ames and James Brooks, as well as to other government members who were directors of the railroad. To avoid impeachment for bribery and fraud five federal judges resigned. Also implicated in the affair were Congressman James A. Garfield, as well as the vice president of the United States, Schuyler Colfax. But neither was ever actually tried, let alone found guilty of any crime, and Garfield went on to become the twentieth president of the United States in 1881. Garfield always insisted he had never bought the ten shares in Crédit Mobilier offered to him and that the several hundred dollars he had received from the company was merely a personal loan.

The Union Pacific officials who were building the railroad got to keep their profits, but much of the land along the railroad right-of-way was returned to the public trust. Later the Speaker of the House of Representatives, James G. Blaine, was rumored to have had some suspicious connections with the Union Pacific Railroad, but these rumors were never confirmed. At the Republican national convention in 1876, Blaine was almost nominated for the presidency. This sudden refurbishing of his reputation and rise to national acclaim was achieved largely on the basis of a statement about Blaine made by famed orator Robert G. Ingersoll, who said: "Like an armed warrior, like a plumed knight, James G. Blaine marched down the halls of the American Congress and threw his shining lance full and fair against the brazen forehead of the defamers of his country and the maligners of his honor." But other conventioneers, harking to the Crédit Mobilier scandal, recalled Blaine being referred to as "the continental liar from the state of Maine" and the "plumed knight" was defeated.

But the convention at which Rutherford B. Hayes was nominated and elected was still several years away. Meanwhile, in 1872, Grant had been nominated for and successfully won a second term as president. To try and shed some of the atmosphere of corruption that had surrounded his administration to date, Grant rid himself of Colfax and chose instead Senator Henry Wilson of Massachusetts as his running mate. Grant easily defeated Democrat Horace Greeley, famed editor of the *New York Tribune*, who campaigned on an honesty-in-government platform. Greeley died less than a month after the election.

Grant had scarcely been inaugurated for a second term in 1873 when a financial panic and depression struck the country. A dissatisfied public soon began to widely criticize the Grant administration, both for its failure to ease the depression and continued corruption in government. In the congressional elections of 1874, Grant's opponents, the Democrats, won a major victory.

Almost at once the new Congress began to investigate a second scandal in the Grant administration. This involved the so-called "Whiskey Ring," which had been originally uncovered by Grant's secretary of the treasury, Benjamin H. Bristow, but the Democrats exploited it. They charged that Bristow had tried to cover up the Whiskey Ring's activities.

In this affair whiskey distillers in St. Louis, Chicago, New York City, and elsewhere had bribed tax officials to get them to cut back on the amount of or to eliminate the federal excise taxes on their products. This practice had defrauded the government of millions of tax dollars. When Grant got word of this affair, he said, "Let no guilty man escape." He would soon have reason to regret these words.

President Grant was brought into the Whiskey Ring scandal when his secretary, General Orville Babcock, was accused of working with Secretary of the Treasury Bristow to cover up the affair. Despite his statement about punishing the guilty, Grant now responded by openly and stoutly defending Babcock—another old army crony—who was eventually cleared of all charges despite strong evidence of his guilt. Several tax collectors were found guilty of defrauding the government, but none of the top leaders was ever punished. Grant did, however, fire Babcock over the Grant family's strong objections.

The Grant administration was still suffering from the severe blows of the Whiskey Ring scandal when Secretary of War William W. Belknap was accused of taking bribes from an agent at a government trading post in Indian territory. (Commissioner of Indian Affairs Parker was not involved in this affair.)

This complicated case involved both Belknap's first wife, Carita, and her sister, Amanda, whom Belknap married when Carita died. Belknap himself was known to be a scrupulously honest man—he had thrown people out of his office for offering him bribes—but apparently Carita and Amanda were somewhat less honest. First Carita and then Amanda accepted cash payments from a man named John Evans to make sure Evans would retain his job as a post trader at Fort Sill, Oklahoma. These payments were made via Caleb Marsh, a family friend, who kept part of the bribe for his own use.

The Evans money that the sisters received amounted to $6,000 a year—a sizable sum in those days—and kept coming for several years. But Amanda was quite extravagant and at one point insisted that Caleb Marsh give her a large cash advance. It is not quite clear what happened at this point, but soon Congress was investigating the long-standing bribe, and the bribe led to Belknap's second wife. This affair, of course, involved Belknap himself, who soon resigned as secretary of war despite his proclaimed innocence.

Grant accepted Belknap's resignation before learning that Belknap had been impeached by Congress. The impeachment trial went forward anyway, but Belknap was acquitted, mainly on the basis that he was no longer a government official. Grant was then severely criticized for prematurely accepting Belknap's resignation.

Weary and sick of defending his administration from charges of corruption, Grant told Congress in his last message to that body: "It was my fortune, or misfortune, to be called to the office of Chief Executive without any previous political training. . . . Under such circumstances it is but reasonable to suppose that errors of judgment must have occurred. . . . Mistakes have been made, as all can see and I admit."

Despite the problems of his administration, Grant still retained much of his popularity when he left the White House. There was even some talk of nominating him for an unprecedented third term. But this was the convention at which the Republicans chose Hayes. In the most closely contested national race in American political history, Hayes defeated his Democratic opponent, Samuel J. Tilden, by one electoral vote. This decision as to who was to be president finally had to be decided by the electoral commission.

Soon after leaving office Grant and his family went on a trip around the world. Everywhere they went they were greeted enthusiastically. When they returned home, Grant and Julia settled in the home in Galena that had been given to them after the Civil War. Again there was talk of nominating Grant for a third presidential term, but Grant was reluctant to face the rigors of the White House once again. He once said: "I was never so glad to leave any place as I was to leave the White House."

After several years in Galena, the Grants moved to a house they bought at 3 East 66th Street in New York City. There they planned to continue a quiet retirement. Unfortunately, Grant's experiences with dishonest businessmen were not over. His son, Ulysses, Jr., was a partner in the banking firm of Grant and Ward and encouraged his father to invest his money there. Ferdinand Ward, young Ulysses told his parents, was a financial genius who would triple their money. Grant Senior ultimately invested his entire savings, about $100,000, there and even encouraged friends to invest their money there too. Within a matter of months, Ward was proved to be a swindler and confidence man who bankrupted the investment firm in 1884, leaving the Grants penniless. Eventually Ward was sentenced to the state penitentiary, but this action did the Grants and their bilked friends little good.

Grant, who had borne all of his ill-fated experiences with untrustworthy people stoically up to this point, now said: "I have made it a rule of my life to trust a man long after other people gave him up, but I don't see how I can ever trust any human being again."

At this point Congress stepped in and restored Grant to the rank of full general so the ex-president would at least have enough money to live on. To earn an additional income, Grant undertook the writing of his experiences in the Civil War for the *Century Magazine*. At about this time Grant began to feel severe pains in his throat, an ailment eventually diagnosed as cancer. The cause was probably the large number of cigars he had smoked—up to twenty a day—since the Civil War.

In explaining how he had acquired the cigar habit, Grant had earlier told his friend, General Horace Porter, "I had been a light smoker previous to the attack on Donelson [this was Fort Donelson, Tennessee, against which Grant successfully led his men in mid-February, 1862]. In the accounts published in the papers, I was represented as smoking a cigar in the midst of the conflict; and many persons, thinking, no doubt, that tobacco was my chief solace, sent me boxes of the choicest brands. As many as ten thousand were soon received. I gave away all I could get rid of, but having such a quantity on hand I naturally smoked more than I would have done under ordinary circumstances, and I have continued the habit ever since."

Grant's war articles in the *Century Magazine* were seen by noted author Samuel Clemens (Mark Twain), who had connections in the publishing business. Twain made arrangements with Grant to have his complete war memoirs published. This contractual arrangement eventually resulted in the Grant family's receiving upwards of $500,000 in royalties.

The completion of Grant's *Personal Memoirs* proved to be a race against death. To escape the summer heat in New York, Grant and Julia moved to Mount McGregor, near Saratoga, in the Adirondacks. There, despite excruciating pain, Grant wrote daily, struggling to complete the telling of his Civil War experiences before he died. Remarkably, he was able to complete his task just a week before his death on July 23, 1885.

Even more remarkable under the circumstances was the quality of the finished *Memoirs*. At the time of their publication in two volumes in 1885 and 1886, they were considered by critics to be a classic and have continued to be so regarded up to the present day. Mark Twain compared them favorably with Caesar's *Commentaries*, and modern military history authority John Keegan has called the *Memoirs* "an enthralling history of one man's generalship, perhaps the most revelatory autobiography of high command to exist in any language."

Grant and his wife Julia are buried in an elaborate tomb erected by the nation on Riverside Drive in New York City.

Section Two

The Harding Administration's Teapot Dome Scandal

Warren G. Harding

3

Warren G. Harding: From Country Editor to President

One historian, Samuel Eliot Morison, has said that the scandals of Grant's administration were equaled only by those of Harding's. And in most ratings of United States presidents by historians, Harding is near or at the bottom of the list.

But Grant himself was a morally upright man, while Harding was morally weak. Although Harding probably had no connection with the infamous Teapot Dome scandal of his administration, it is now known that despite the fact that he was a married man he carried on love affairs with two other women. One of these women was married to a friend of Harding's; the other was a teenager when he first knew her and by whom he probably had a daughter.

Warren Gamaliel Harding, twenty-ninth president of the United States, was born on a farm in rural Morrow County, Ohio, near Corsica (later Blooming Grove) on November 2, 1865, the last year of the Civil War. He was the oldest of eight children born to George and Phoebe Harding.

During much of Harding's life there was a rumor that one of his ancestors—it was never clear which one—was black. An early biographer, Wiliam E. Chancellor, also claimed that Harding's schoolboy nickname was "Nig" because of his dark complexion. At times during his life Harding himself wondered aloud if there could be any truth in the rumor that he was a mulatto. The rumor, however, was never substantiated.

Harding's father dabbled in several enterprises to support his large family, one of them being his practice as a doctor of homeopathic medicine. Homeopathy, which has never been widely practiced in the United States, is a method of treating disease by giving small doses of drugs that in a healthy person would cause symptoms like those of the disease. Another of the senior Harding's business efforts was as part owner of a weekly newspaper, *The Caledonia Argus*. Young Warren took an early interest in the newspaper business while working on the *Argus* as an apprentice printer and pressman.

While still in his early teens, Warren attended Ohio Central College at Iberia, from which he was graduated in 1882. At seventeen Warren tried teaching school for $30 a month but soon gave it up as too difficult. "The toughest job I ever had," he later said. He then moved back with his mother and father, who by this time were living in Marion, Ohio, where his father was still trying his hand at a variety of mostly unsuccessful business efforts. Warren himself dabbled at studying law and selling insurance and then went to work as a reporter for the weekly *Marion Democratic Mirror*. His salary: $1 a week. He only earned the dollar a week for a few weeks, however, because he loudly announced his political support for Republican presidential candidate James G. Blaine. As a result, young Harding's Democratic boss fired him.

Harding and two of his friends, John Sickel and Jack Warwick, then scraped together several hundred dollars and bought the bankrupt daily newspaper, the *Marion Star*. His partners soon dropped out of the publishing venture, but young Harding kept at it and eventually became a financial success.

One of the main reasons for Harding's early newspaper success— and later political success for that matter—was his wife, Florence, whom he called "Duchess." Harding was twenty-five and Florence Kling DeWolfe thirty when they were married. She was the divorcée daughter of a wealthy Marion banker, Amos Kling. Her father disapproved of her first marriage and refused to support his daughter when she was abandoned by her husband. In obtaining her divorce, Florence legally retained her maiden name.

To support herself, Florence gave piano lessons, and one of her pupils was Harding's sister, Chat. It was through Chat that Florence met the young editor of the *Star*. At this time Harding was a tall, handsome young man with a touch of gray hair that added to his distinguished good looks. Soon she was determined to marry him, and when Florence Kling made up her mind about something, there was usually no changing it. Harding, on his part, was flattered by Florence's attention and was certainly not unaware of her father's wealth. But Amos Kling would have nothing to do with the financially struggling Harding, once denouncing him as "a fortune-hunting nigger" when they met in the local courthouse and threatening to kill him. Nevertheless, on July 9, 1891, the *Star* reported the marriage of Warren Harding and Florence Kling, which had taken place on the previous day.

At the time the Hardings were married, Warren had turned the *Star* into a respected Ohio newspaper, but it was not very successful financially. Florenced turned things around. She took over as business manager, and almost immediately the *Star* became a hugely profitable enterprise.

The Duchess also pushed her husband to succeed beyond the boundaries of Marion. Politics seemed the natural outlet for Harding with his great good looks and hail-fellow-well-met manner. In this effort the Duchess was soon aided by a wily Ohio political kingmaker, Harry M. Daugherty.

Locally Harding, as editor of the *Star*, was frequently called upon to give speeches, and he soon developed into an excellent orator. He also was made a director of various business companies, as well as a trustee of the Trinity Baptist Church. Thus, he now had an impeccable background for his entry into politics.

In 1898 Harding was elected a Republican state senator. In 1903 he became the state's lieutenant governor but lost a bid for state governor in 1910. But by this time he had become acquainted with Daugherty, a turning point in Harding's life.

Harry M. Daugherty (the named was pronounced "Dokerty") had also served in the Ohio state legislature as a Republican representative but at the time he and Harding met was a lobbyist for several large corporations. After their first meeting Daugherty reportedly commented, "What a great-looking president he'd make!" The remark was appropriate as well as prophetic. Harding somewhat resembled a noble Roman senator, and his good looks would help carry him to the White House.

Urged on by Daugherty and the Duchess, a reluctant Harding ran for the U.S. Senate in 1914. Somewhat to his own surprise, he won the Republican nomination and then went on to defeat the Democratic candidate by a slim margin.

Harding's career as a U.S. senator was undistinguished, but he thoroughly enjoyed his term in what he proudly regarded as "the most exclusive club in the world." Although he himself drank, Harding did publicly favor the Eighteenth Amendment to the Constitution, which prohibited the manufacture, sale, and transportation of alcoholic beverages. This amendment was ratified on January 29, 1919. He also publicly favored giving women the right to vote, and the Nineteenth Amendment (woman suffrage) was ratified on August 26, 1920. Actually Harding was not personally in favor of either of these amendments but backed them to curry favor with political leaders.

This attitude, aided by Daugherty's constant efforts on his behalf, continued to pay off for Harding. In 1916 he was the keynote speaker at the Republican convention that nominated Charles Evans Hughes for the presidency. Although Hughes was defeated by Woodrow Wilson, Harding's keynote address and the man who made it were not forgotten by the delegates to the Republican convention in Chicago in 1920.

It was while Harding was in Washington, D.C., as a senator that he and Nan Britton began their long-term love affair. Thirty years younger than Harding, Nan had known Harding since she was a teenager back in Marion. There she had seen the handsome Harding striding past her parents' home on his way to and from work and had formed a schoolgirl "crush" on him. This youthful infatuation—Nan was fourteen when she first decided she was in love with Harding—continued through her high school years. So serious did it become that both her mother and father spoke with her about it. Her father, who knew Harding quite well, also spoke to him about Nan's infatuation, so Harding was well aware of the young lady's feelings for him. Once or twice he ran into her on the street and stopped to chat casually with her, but their relationship went no farther than that at that time. When Harding ran for public office, she plastered her bedroom with pictures and posters of him, so all of her girlfriends knew of the crush too. Eventually word of it got back to the Duchess, and she too spoke firmly with her husband about it.

Soon after Harding assumed his Senate seat, he was surprised to receive a letter from Nan Britton, who was then twenty, asking him for a job. Harding responded by making an appointment with her in New York, where she was attending a secretarial school. He met her there and told her he had no job for her in Washington but that he would help support her in New York. Their affair began soon afterward with Harding managing to see her once a week. In addition, when he had speaking engagements at various towns and cities in the Midwest, he paid her rail fare to meet him. Usually he registered her as his niece, and they had separate but adjoining rooms.

When Harding began his affair with Nan, he was already carrying on an affair of long standing with Carrie Philips, the wife of his friend, James Philips. The most beautiful young woman in Marion, Carrie began her liaison with Harding several years before he went to Washington. Carrie and her husband and Harding and his wife had been neighbors who visited back and forth in each other's homes.

Following the death of their infant son, Carrie and Jim seemed to drift apart rather than grow closer together. The Hardings did their best to console Carrie, who seemed especially heartbroken. Then one weekend when both Mrs. Harding and Jim Philips were out of town, Harding paid a call on Carrie Philips by himself. Their love affair began that day and continued for some fifteen years, ending only when Harding became a candidate for president in 1920.

According to legend, Harding's nomination for the presidency was decided by a small group of politicians led by Harry Daugherty, who gathered together in a smoke-filled room in Chicago during the Repubican convention in 1920 and there named Harding as the candidate. The smoke-filled-room legend began with a post-convention story in *The New York Times* that said Harry Daugherty had predicted the nomination outcome. According to the *Times*, Daugherty had stated even before the convention began that "at the proper time . . . some fifteen men, bleary-eyed with loss of sleep and perspiring profusely with the excessive heat, will sit down in seclusion around a big table. I will present the name of Senator Harding to them, and before we get through they will put him over."

There turned out to be just enough truth in Daugherty's prediction to make it stand up over the years, and until the adoption of the system of nationwide primaries that is in operation today, the media continued to talk about presidential nominations being decided in smoke-filled rooms at every national convention.

Following his usual pattern, Harding was reluctant to run for president, stating that the Senate was far more to his liking. But once again the Duchess and Daugherty combined forces and persuaded him to become a candidate.

When the convention began in June of 1920, Harding had already been mentioned as a possible candidate, but he was far from being the favorite. In fact, the favorites were Governor Frank O. Lowden of Illinois, former U.S. Army Chief of Staff Major General Leonard Wood, and Senator Hiram W. Johnson of California. But working behind the scenes was the tireless Harry Daugherty, who managed to meet most of the delegates and suggest to them his man, Senator Warren Harding, as a possible alternate choice if there was a deadlock.

And a deadlock there was. To meet just such an eventuality, Daugherty had rented a room at the Blackstone Hotel. Key Republicans did meet there, and Daugherty pointed out to them that Harding would be a powerful vote-getter and an ideal compromise candidate because he could heal the wounds suffered by the backers of any and all other defeated candidates. In a skillful job of public relations, Daugherty and his aides also passed this word among all of the convention delegates, reminding them too of Harding's great gifts as a speaker. The technique proved to be 100 percent effective, and when the convention resumed its sessions and the deadlock continued, Harding was finally chosen as the presidential nominee. Calvin Coolidge, governor of Massachusetts, was chosen as his vice presidential running mate.

The night before the actual nomination, when it appeared that Harding stood a good chance of being the nominee, one of the Republican party stalwarts, George Harvey, called on him in his room and formally asked him "whether there is anything that might be brought up against you that would embarrass the party, any impediment that might disqualify or make you inexpedient, either as a candidate or as president."

Within a matter of minutes Harding told Harvey no, there was no such impediment.

Harding made this declaration despite the fact that his affair with Carrie Philips had not yet ended and his affair with Nan Britton was in full bloom. In fact, Nan was now living with her sister in Chicago, and the sister was helping to care for Nan's recently born baby daughter, Elizabeth Ann, whose father, Nan said, was Warren Harding—a claim that Harding then nor later made no effort to deny, although no public acknowledgment of the fact was made.

During the convention, despite the press of politics and despite the fact that the Duchess had accompanied her husband on this trip, Harding managed to break away several times and visit with Nan for an hour or two. He also continued to support her and Elizabeth Ann even after he got into the White House.

An interesting sidelight regarding Harding's nomination was the fact that several months before the convention his wife, along with several other senators' wives, visited an astrologer, Madam Marcia, in Washington. The Duchess did not give Madam Marcia her husband's name or occupation, but she did give her Harding's birth date, November 2, 1865, and other vital statistics. Madam Marcia, who undoubtedly knew from her own sources who Mrs. Harding was, as well as the identity of the man she was talking about, told the Duchess that if the man in question was considering running for president, he would definitely be nominated and elected. "But," she warned, "he will not live through his term . . . I see sudden, violent, or peculiar death."

It was not merely that the astrologer's prediction proved to be true that made it interesting in the light of history. More than half a century later the wife of another president would also consult an astrologer about her husband, and these consultations would result in headlines in newspapers across the country. This was Nancy Reagan, wife of President Ronald Reagan, whose own administration was not exactly scandal free, as is discussed later in this book.

To oppose Harding in the 1920 national election, the Democrats nominated Governor James M. Cox of Ohio as their presidential candidate and Assistant Secretary of the Navy Franklin D. Roosevelt as their vice presidential candidate.

Harding conducted what he called a "front porch campaign." He did very little campaign traveling but remained at home in Marion, where he made speeches that were printed in newspapers throughout the country and greeted various political delegations. Television had not yet been invented and radio was in its infancy, so newspapers and word-of-mouth were the major means of national communication.

However, for the first time in history, the presidential election returns were broadcast on November 2, when station KDKA in Pittsburgh announced Harding's victory over Cox by a large margin—more than sixteen million votes to just over nine million. Later Harding also became the first president to have a speech broadcast over the radio when he dedicated the Francis Scott Key Memorial at Baltimore, Maryland's, Fort McHenry on June 14, 1922. Key, of course, was the author of "The Star Spangled Banner," which he had composed after watching the night-long British bombardment of Fort McHenry in the War of 1812.

Harding's affair with Carrie Philips was finally broken off before he was elected president. Despite Harding's earlier statement that there was nothing potentially scandalous in his personal life, several members of the Republican National Committee got wind of his relationship with Mrs. Philips and decided it had to be broken off. They sent an emissary to Marion to talk not only with Carrie but also with Jim Philips, who by now also knew of the affair. The emissary agreed to pay Carrie Philips a lump sum of $20,000, plus a monthly fee as long as Harding was in office. In addition, she and her husband were to take an expenses-paid world tour. The single stipulation was that Carrie and Jim leave before the election and stay away until after it was over. They agreed and left before the summer was out.

But Harding did not break off his affair with Nan Britton. He continued to see her all the time he was in the White House, even on occasion inviting her to Washington when the Duchess was away. As a go-between to carry messages and money to Nan and to receive messages from her, Harding used secret service agents and his valet. Many of the details about the continued liaison between Nan Britton and the president did not become generally known until long after Harding's death when Nan wrote and had privately published in 1927 a confessional account of their affair entitled *The President's Daughter*. In addition to relating the straightforward facts about being the mother of Harding's daughter, Nan supplied such lurid details as their having made love in the galoshes-littered cloakroom adjoining the president's office. *The President's Daughter* was, for many months, a national best-seller, although it was sold from under the counter in most bookstores.

But the Nan Britton affair was successfully kept under wraps until after the Teapot Dome scandal broke. Meanwhile, along the way a few other problems raised their ugly heads during the Harding administration.

4

The Harding Administration

Like Grant, Harding brought with him to Washington a number of old friends and cronies. These whiskey-drinking, poker-playing buddies were widely known as "the Ohio gang." But Harding was also shrewd enough to name some sound men as his aides.

To begin with, of course, he had a morally straitlaced and hardheaded businessman administrator in his vice president, Calvin Coolidge. Coolidge had made a name for himself nationally when as governor of Massachusetts he had put a quick end to a Boston police strike by calling out the state guard. When labor leader Samuel Gompers protested, Coolidge stated flatly: "There is no right to strike against the public safety by anybody, anywhere, any time."

Harding insisted that Coolidge attend all cabinet meetings. He was the first vice president to do so.

Also among the outstanding cabinet members Harding selected were Secretary of State Charles Evans Hughes, a renowned lawyer and future chief justice of the Supreme Court; Secretary of Agriculture Henry C. Wallace, highly regarded editor of the national magazine *Wallace's Farmer*; Secretary of Commerce Herbert Hoover, internationally known engineer and future U.S. president; Secretary of the Treasury Andrew W. Mellon, highly reputable American banker; and Postmaster General Will H. Hays, future czar of the motion picture industry.

Two cabinet members who would eventually help disgrace the Harding administration were Secretary of the Interior Albert B. Fall of New Mexico and Attorney General Harry M. Daugherty of Ohio. Fall had been a Senate crony of Harding's and, most significant of all, was closely allied with a number of millionaire oilmen who had contributed heavily to Harding's campaign. Daugherty had little to recommend him as attorney general, but the fact that he had master-minded Harding's presidential campaign meant he had to be rewarded in some fashion.

A kind of unofficial member of the Harding cabinet was a man named Jesse Smith. Smith too was a Harding crony whose sole claim on the president was the shared love for poker, as his faithful atten-dance at the card-playing sessions attested. These sessions were held at what was called "The Little Green House" on K Street, which the Ohio gang took over as their headquarters. Political favors were also dispensed from here by Daugherty and his pal Smith.

The liquor consumed at the K Street gatherings was, of course, bootleg or illegal liquor since the prohibition law was now in effect. But in obtaining liquor illegally, Harding and his cronies were not out of step with the rest of the nation. Bootleggers and speakeasies—un-licensed clubs where liquor could be secretly obtained—were widely patronized by the American public. Underworld criminals who made possible the prohibited sale of alcohol soon developed into the widespread national crime syndicate that is still with us today but now specializes in the illegal distribution of drugs other than alcohol.

In general, the widespread relaxation of public morals was not unlike that during the Grant administration. In Grant's day the public was eager to relax after the trials and self-denial of the Civil War; in Harding's era there was a post-World War I atmosphere of "back to normalcy," as Harding called it. "Normalcy" soon grew into what was more commonly known as the freedom and license of the "Roaring Twenties" with the attitude of "anything goes," which was the virtual slogan of the times.

For about a year after Harding's inauguration on March 4, 1921—the first inauguration to be described over the radio—things went relatively smoothly in his administration. But already behind the scenes the schemers and illegal operators were at work. One of the places where they were most active was in the Veterans' Bureau, which was headed by Charles R. Forbes.

Following the end of World War I on November 11, 1918, there was an enormous amount of war surplus material left over in various warehouses around the United States. Word reached Harding late in 1922 that this material was being secretly sold at a price well below its market value. Despite the fact that Forbes was touted as a World War I hero—others said he had been a deserter—he was asked to resign by Harding and was replaced by General Frank T. Hines. A short time later Charles F. Cramer, a Veterans' Bureau attorney, committed suicide. The Senate then launched an investigation of the Veterans' Bureau, and eventually Forbes was brought to trial, found guilty, fined $10,000, and sentenced to two years in prison.

During these disclosures Jesse Smith was sharing an apartment in Washington with Attorney General Daugherty. Although he had always acted legally, he claimed, in dispensing patronage jobs from the house on K Street, Smith was apparently aware that some sort of scandal was about to reach him, and he shot and killed himself in the apartment. The Harding administration blamed Smith's suicide on ill health.

By the spring of 1923, President Harding was a deeply troubled chief executive. His woes were compounded by the fact that the country was suffering from an economic depression. As a result, the Republicans had slipped badly in the fall 1922 congressional elections. To try and restore confidence in his administration, Harding, his wife, and a number of aides made a tour by railroad train and boat across the country and up into Canada and Alaska. This was the first presidential tour of the latter two places.

The "Voyage of Understanding," which Harding called this trip, began in late June of 1923. When the train stopped for a layover in Kansas City, the deeply worried Harding was further troubled after a visit from the wife of his now former Secretary of the Interior Albert Fall. In the midst of all the charges and allegations against high government officials that had been flying around Washington, Fall had resigned. He had not made the reason clear, and it is possible that that is what Mrs. Fall and the president talked about.

A week or so later Harding was even more disturbed when a long message in code from Washington, D.C., reached him in Alaska, where they had traveled by boat, the S.S. *Henderson*. Probably from Mrs. Fall and most certainly from the coded message, Harding learned for the first time of Fall's involvement in leasing government reserve oil fields to commercial oil companies. Although he did not specifically divulge what was troubling him, Harding did ask his aides what a man was supposed to do when all of his friends betrayed him. Actually the Senate had already begun an investigation of Fall's bribe-taking, an investigation that would eventually lead to a trial and a verdict that would send Fall to jail.

Fall's alleged misdeeds centered around two government-owned oil reserves. One of these was at Elk Hills, California, and the other was about fifty miles north of Casper, Wyoming, and known—because of its shape—as Teapot Dome. These reserves were established around the beginning of the twentieth century when the U.S. Navy had switched from coal to oil to fuel its ships. First, President William Howard Taft officially designated the Elk Hills area as an oil reserve in 1912. Then in 1915 President Woodrow Wilson designated Teapot Dome as a reserve. In both instances the reserves were put under the specific control of the secretary of the navy.

Then the Harding administration and Secretary of the Interior Fall entered the picture.

Fall was an anticonservationist. The only public lands that should be in the hands of the government, he thought, were the national parks. All other public lands, in his opinion, should be in private hands. As far as the oil reserves were concerned, Fall firmly believed they never should have been created.

One of the reasons for Fall's anticonservationist views was the fact that he owned one of the nation's largest ranches, Three Rivers Ranch, in New Mexico. But some of the thousands of acres Fall controlled were leased from the state and others were actually public lands to which he had laid claim. In utilizing the public lands to which he had laid claim, Fall had borrowed heavily to improve them, as well as to buy additional property and herds of cattle to graze on that property. In fact, when Fall became secretary of the interior, he had bank debts of almost $150,000 and had not paid taxes on his ranch for some eight years.

One of Fall's first moves as secretary of the interior was to take over control of the naval oil reserves from Edwin Denby. Secretary Denby told President Harding that he did not think the Navy should be responsible for these reserves and that they should be in the hands of the Department of the Interior. How much if any arm-twisting by Fall was necessary to get Denby to make this move has never been clear. In any event, Harding apparently agreed, and the transfer was made by executive order—the draft for which was drawn up by Fall.

Fall always claimed that in all of his operations with the oil reserves he acted as the Navy's agent and in the Navy's best interests. But several high-ranking naval officers objected strenuously to the transfer and said so in no uncertain terms. Their objections went unheeded.

Interestingly, the U.S. Navy high command had for some years been speculating on the possibility of war with Japan over control of the Pacific. To prepare for such an eventuality, the Navy wanted large oil reserve facilities, including huge storage tanks, constructed and maintained not only on the West Coast of the United States but also at Pearl Harbor, Hawaii—and the date was almost half a century before Japan actually attacked Pearl Harbor to bring the United States into World War II.

In Fall's defense it must be said that he made every effort to establish these oil reserve facilities just as the Navy wanted them. But along the way he apparently cut a few corners and took at least one huge bribe.

The major difficulty Fall faced as soon as the Department of the Interior took over the Elk Hills and Teapot Dome reserves was how to solve the problem of major oil companies drilling wells near the reserves and draining them of their oil. Fortunes, of course, were being made in the early business of exploration and exploitation of new fields, and few holds were barred in these pioneer get-rich-quick battles between the future oil barons. Not only the navies of the world but also major industries were scrambling for "black gold."

Earlier presidential administrations had failed to solve the problem of so-called "seepage" from oil reserves. They had, in fact, compounded the problem by leasing certain areas near and even within the oil reserves themselves. The commercial companies willingly paid the government fees for these leases, but the fees were modest in comparison to oil company profits.

Fall decided to continue and even to expand these leasing arrangements, but he added a new twist to the deal. Rather than taking cash royalty payments, the government would take certificates entitling the Navy to petroleum products—fuel oil and gasoline—at discounts, plus the agreement by the oil companies to construct steel tanks wherever the Navy chose to have them built along the U.S. coast.

In this way, Fall claimed, the government would be getting the greatest value from its oil reserves. The Navy was agreeable because with the pacifist postwar mood that prevailed throughout the country, Congress was not about to vote funds to expand naval fuel storage facilities or to provide for any other military preparedness.

Under this agreement in April of 1922, Fall leased the whole of the Teapot Dome reserve for twenty years to Harry F. Sinclair, president of the Sinclair Oil Company. The royalties in kind that Sinclair agreed to ranged from 12-1/2 to 50 percent, depending upon how productive the wells were. Who was to decide this productivity value was not clear.

Fall did not conduct any competitive bidding for the Teapot Dome Reserve drilling rights. He did not do so, he said, because "to call attention to the fact that contracts providing for enormous storages for future use in crisis of oil . . . involved national security."

This would not be the last time both an anticonservationist would be put in charge of the nation's resources and "national security" would be used as a cover-up for apparent wrongdoing. Both would be echoed in the Reagan administration.

Shortly after making the Sinclair agreement, Fall also turned over rights to a lease of the entire Elk Hills reserve—about 30,000 acres—to Edward Doheny and his Pan American Petroleum and Transport Company of California. In return, Doheny and his company agreed to the construction of oil storage tanks at Pearl Harbor. In addition, for an immediate payment of six million barrels of crude oil from the Elk Hills reserve, Doheny agreed to dredge a channel into Pearl Harbor and build docks and wharves to accommodate oil tankers as well as U.S. Navy battleships.

Technically, Fall had not disobeyed the law in leasing both the Elk Hills and Teapot Dome reserves. Actually, however, he had privately taken money from both Sinclair and Doheny. This money came as a "loan" of almost $400,000. It probably did not seem much to either of the two multimillionaires, but it more than helped keep Fall in the ranching business. Not only could he pay off his bank loans, but he also could catch up on his tax delinquencies.

Fall always claimed that the money he received from Sinclair and Doheny had absolutely nothing to do with the granting of the oil leases. Unfortunately for him, he went one step further. When he resigned as secretary of the interior and Congress began to investigate his activities, Fall wrote a letter to the Senate investigating committee stating flatly that he had never received a dime from either Sinclair or Doheny. Later it was proved that this letter was a lie, and Fall was tried, found guilty of taking a bribe, and sentenced to a year in jail.

When Harding received the coded cable informing him of the

Senate's investigation of Fall, Harding's first exclamation was one of disbelief. "If Albert Fall isn't an honest man, I'm not fit to be President of the United States."

But Harding's statement may merely have been a show of bravado in the face of the facts about his crumbling administration. In any event, as the Harding party returned to the United States (Alaska was not yet a state), Harding was visibly a shaken man. Soon he was a mortally ill man.

Harding first became ill in Seattle, Washington, where it was thought he was suffering from indigestion due to bad seafood. But as he grew steadily worse, doctors called in by Harding's personal physician, Dr. Charles Sawyer, feared it was something more serious. As a result, the Harding train was ordered straight through to San Francisco. There the president was put to bed in a suite at the Palace Hotel. His wife had a suite just across the hall.

For a day or two Harding showed marked signs of recovery. But then, on the evening of August 2, 1923, after a visit with the Duchess, his nurse found him dead.

Dr. Sawyer gave the cause of death as a cerebral hemorrhage, but consulting doctors disagreed. However, Mrs. Harding refused to permit an autopsy, so the specific cause of death was never really known. This fact, plus the scandals that had begun to erupt and continued to erupt around the dead president, caused all kinds of wild rumors to be circulated. One wild-eyed author, Gaston B. Means, even went so far as to claim in his book *The Strange Death of President Harding* that Mrs. Harding had poisoned her husband to prevent his impeachment and disgrace. Means, however, was a generally disreputable scandal-monger who eventually wound up in jail for accepting $100,000 for spuriously claiming he had knowledge about the kidnapping of the baby of famed flier Charles A. Lindberg and his wife Anne in March 1932. Means was sentenced to fifteen years in prison at Fort Leavenworth, Kansas, where he died. The money was never recovered.

While it was mainly Means's book that gave rise to all of the rumors about President Harding's "mysterious" death—rumors that still persist today—Mrs. Harding's actions following her husband's passing certainly strengthened these rumors. Not only did she refuse to allow an autopsy, but she also did her best to destroy all of Harding's private papers both in Washington and Marion, so that biographers and historians have since had the greatest difficulty in reconstructing the events of Harding's life.

At the time of Harding's death, the full fury of the Teapot Dome scandal had not yet broken, and Harding was still much beloved by the American public. Consequently, the train bearing his remains that traveled across the nation from the West Coast to Washington and then to Marion was greeted all along its route by throngs of sorrowing spectators. This outpouring of interest and apparent affection for the president was reminiscent of the public's reaction following Abraham Lincoln's assassination and the return of his body to Springfield, Illinois. Harding was buried in a special tomb in Marion, where his wife's body was also laid to rest just a little over a year later. The Duchess died on November 21, 1924, at Marion.

It was not too long after Harding's burial that the Senate investigation led by Senator Thomas Walsh of Montana began to disclose the unsavory details of Albert Fall and his Teapot Dome manipulations. This scandal carried over clear into the 1930s. In 1929 Fall finally received his one year's jail sentence and was imprisoned in 1931-32.

The second major figure to bring disgrace to the Harding administration, Harry Daugherty, never spent a day in jail. In fact, he frequently boasted, "No charge against me was ever proven in any court." The boast would be echoed by Edwin Meese, President Ronald Reagan's attorney general, who also was frequently accused but never found guilty of any wrongdoing.

Daugherty during his relatively brief term as attorney general was twice the subject of Senate investigations. Both were led by Montana Senator Burton K. Wheeler. They centered around why Daugherty had

57

not prosecuted the key figures in the early scandals regarding World War I surplus sales by the Veterans' Bureau. Daugherty flatly refused to cooperate with the Senate investigating committee, and Calvin Coolidge, who had succeeded Harding as president, then asked Daugherty to resign as attorney general.

After his resignation from the cabinet, Daugherty was finally indicted for malfeasance. He was indicted and twice brought to trial because, it was claimed, he had taken bribes while he was in office. But since he was now out of office and the statute of limitations had run out on his alleged crimes, all he could be accused of was failing to provide "honest, impartial, and unprejudiced services and judgment" as attorney general. He was not found guilty in either trial due to hung juries.

Both Fall and Daugherty lived on into the 1940s, both protesting their innocence until they died. Their deaths, however, were little noticed since the United States was then deeply involved in fighting World War II—a war against evil and corruption of another kind, that of totalitarianism and dictatorship.

Section 3

The Nixon Administration's Watergate Scandal

Richard M. Nixon

5

Richard M. Nixon: From Young Lawyer to President

When Richard Nixon was a boy of eleven, the newspapers were filled with stories about Teapot Dome and the scandals during the Harding administration. The stories angered the young Nixon. In fact, he told his mother, to whom he had already confessed his ambitions to go into public service, "When I grow up, I'll be a lawyer who can't be bribed."

Although Nixon did grow up to be an honest lawyer and eventually the thirty-seventh president of the United States, unfortunately the Nixon administration would conclude with a scandal every bit as big as if not bigger than any during the Harding administration. The so-called "Watergate scandal" or "Watergate affair" would result in Nixon's being the first U.S. president ever to resign from office. Neither Grant nor Harding apparently took any part in the scandals during their administrations. Nixon, however, did play an active role in at least the "cover-up" aspect of the Watergate affair. It was this that drove him from office.

Richard Milhous Nixon was born in Yorba Linda, a small farming town in California, on January 9, 1913. He was the second of five sons born to Francis Anthony Nixon and Hannah Milhous Nixon. After an attempt to run a lemon grove at Yorba Linda failed, the Nixon family moved to nearby Whittier, which was Mrs. Nixon's home town. There the father, Francis or Frank Nixon, ran a combination gasoline station and grocery store, where young Richard worked as a boy.

Frank Nixon had a strong interest in politics, which greatly influenced Richard. In both grade school and high school Richard was active in debates for which his father helped him prepare. Years later one of Richard's former debate coaches told political historian Theodore White that she remembered young Dick Nixon and respected his quality—she simply did not like him . . . . "There was something mean in him," she went on, "mean in the way he put his questions, argued his points. Dick's father," she remembered, "was mean too . . . . His temper frightened people." In this early assessment of young Dick Nixon, the child seemed to be father of the man.

But most of the family's extracurricular activity was not involved with debates. It was involved in local Quaker religious affairs. Mrs. Nixon was a devout Quaker, and she prevailed upon her family to attend services at the local meetinghouse several times on Sundays as well as at least once during the week. Richard also played the church organ. He became especially close to his mother and shared her church dedication after two of his brothers died at an early age.

Young Nixon attended Whittier College, also a Quaker institution. There he continued to be extremely industrious. He was both president of his freshman class and later president of the student body. His debate activity also continued, and his grades were excellent. At athletics he was not so successful, never advancing beyond the second team in football. In 1934 Richard graduated second in his class from Whittier and was awarded a scholarship to study law at Duke University in Durham, North Carolina.

At Duke Nixon was also a hard-working, ambitious student. He was first elected president of the student body and then president of the Duke Student Bar Association. In 1937 Nixon graduated from law school third in his class. Shortly after his graduation Nixon passed the California bar examination and joined a law firm in Whittier.

In addition to practicing law, Nixon was active in Whittier's little theater group. There he met Thelma Patricia Ryan, a teacher in the local high school. After going together for two years, Pat and Richard Nixon were married on June 21, 1940.

By this time World War II had begun in Europe. When the United States entered the war, Nixon joined the Navy, was commissioned a lieutenant junior grade, and went off to serve as an operations officer with the South Pacific Combat Air Transport Command. By the time the Japanese surrendered in 1945, Nixon had become a lieutenant commander.

Nixon returned to California after the war and decided to go into politics. The first political office he sought was that of U.S. congressman. He ran on the Republican ticket. His opponent was Democrat Jerry Voorhis, who had served in Congress since 1936. In his very first political campaign for national office, Nixon chose a theme that would stand him in good stead for the rest of his political career. This was anti-Communism. For the first time Nixon also showed a facet of his personality that he would continue to demonstrate in future political battles. This was a ruthless, one-sided, slashing campaign technique that did not always closely adhere to the facts about his opponent.

Voorhis had once been an outspoken liberal but had grown more and more conservative. Nevertheless, Nixon's campaign rhetoric implied that Voorhis was somehow allied with the Communists because a liberal California political action committee had endorsed Voorhis. Smearing him with the Communist brush succeeded, and Nixon won quite handily on November 5, 1946.

The Nixons then moved to Washington, D.C., with their daughter Patricia, who had been born during the campaign on February 21, 1946. A second daughter, Julie, would be born on July 5, 1948.

Because of his staunch anti-Communist reputation, freshman congressman Nixon was assigned to the House of Representatives Un-American Committee (HUAC), and after a brief period of marking time, it was as a staunch anti-Communist that Nixon's reputation grew. Now, however, he was performing on a national stage.

In mid-1948 a former U.S. State Department official, Alger Hiss, was accused of being a spy for the Soviet Union. His accuser was Whitaker Chambers, himself a self-confessed former spy and now a *Time* magazine editor, who claimed that Hiss had given him State Department secrets to pass along to Russia. Hiss stoutly defended himself before the HUAC, but the dogged Nixon did not let the matter drop with Hiss's denials, although other members of the committee were inclined to believe Hiss's declaration of innocence.

Nixon, working with Chambers, produced enough evidence against Hiss to indicate the former state department employee was guilty. The most damning piece of evidence was a microfilm containing secret material. To keep the microfilm and other classified materials from being discovered, Chambers had hidden them in a hollowed-out pumpkin on his Maryland farm. When this information was revealed, the so-called "Pumpkin Papers" made headline news across the country, and Nixon as well as the two central figures in the spy scandal became nationally famous.

Late in 1948 Hiss was indicted for perjury by a federal grand jury. It took two more years and two trials before Hiss was convicted and given a five-year prison sentence early in 1950. Hiss continued to claim he was innocent, but the damning Chambers' evidence never was discredited.

With his newly won national reputation, Nixon next decided to run for the U.S. Senate. His opponent in this race was a liberal favorite, Helen Gahagan Douglas. Nixon changed his tried and true campaign technique not a whit. He smeared Democrat Douglas with the Communist brush, just as he had smeared Jerry Voorhis, and was equally successful. Nixon won the senatorial campaign on November 7, 1950, by three-quarters of a million votes. At age thirty-eight Nixon became the youngest senator in that session of Congress.

Nixon, for the most part, remained discreetly in the background as a freshman senator. He did, however, continue to hammer away at the Communists. His new target was what he claimed were the

Soviet-supported northern forces in the war in Korea, where the United States and other United Nations troops were supporting South Korea. Nixon also flailed away at the Democratic administration and its leader, Harry S. Truman, who was then president. Nixon claimed that there were still Communists and Communist sympathizers in the Truman government despite the best efforts of HUAC to eliminate them. This crusade was to continue.

In 1952 Dwight D. Eisenhower, famed military leader of the victorious Allied forces in Europe during World War II, was nominated for president by the Republican party. Eisenhower, or "Ike" as he was popularly known, chose Nixon as his vice presidential running mate. This dark horse selection came as somewhat of a surprise to most Republican leaders, and within a few days they were urging Ike to dump Nixon. What was more, Ike was seriously considering doing just that.

The reason for Nixon's sudden fall into national disfavor was a newspaper story in the *New York Post* headlined: SECRET RICH MAN'S TRUST FUND KEEPS NIXON IN STYLE FAR BEYOND HIS SALARY. The dirty campaign chickens had now come home to roost right in Nixon's backyard. And Ike, who had proudly announced Nixon as his running mate, now, not so proudly, let Nixon sink or swim on his own. While the vice presidential nominee announced that he would present his case directly to the public in a national television broadcast, Ike indicated he himself was now just another member of the public who would have to be convinced of Nixon's innocence. "Nixon," Ike said, "will have to prove he is as clean as a hound's tooth."

Nixon came through the trial by public opinion with flying colors in a melodramatic TV performance that went into the history books as the "Checkers Speech." When it was over, a grinning Ike greeted Nixon with open arms and the declaration, "Dick, you're my boy."

The Checkers Speech was made on September 23, 1952. In it Nixon admitted there had indeed been a fund collected by a number of businessmen, but not a penny of this $18,000 fund had been used by him personally. All of it, he insisted, had been spent on his political campaign. He even went so far as to list all of the family assets, including his wife's coat—not a fur but a "plain cloth coat."

The most memorable part of his speech came when he pointed out that during his Senate campaign someone had given the Nixons a cocker spaniel puppy named Checkers. "The kids love Checkers," Nixon said, "and I don't think they should have to give him up." He also went on to say that he didn't think he should quit as the vice presidential nominee "because I am not a quitter." He then invited viewers to call or write their local TV stations to say whether or not they agreed with Nixon. In the next few days phone calls and mail flooded in, almost all of it pro-Nixon. Needless to say, Nixon had triumphed.

In the November election Ike and Nixon won by a landslide over their Democrat opponents, Governor Adlai Stevenson of Illinois and Senator John J. Sparkman of Alabama. Interestingly, the Democratic presidential nominee also had a political slush fund donated by Midwest businessmen. The fund was similar to that of Nixon's, but nothing much was ever made of the Stevenson fund by the media.

Nixon served for eight years as vice president, he and Ike being reelected to their respective offices in 1956. Nixon was mainly occupied during these eight years in filling the largely ceremonial duties of his office, although Ike did his best to make Nixon an involved vice president. Eisenhower included Nixon in all cabinet meetings and had Nixon preside over cabinet meetings when the president was not in Washington. This experience stood the nation in good stead because on the several occasions when the president was seriously ill, Nixon was able to take over the leadership reins without a hitch. Ike had a heart attack in 1955, an operation for an intestinal ailment in 1956, and a mild stroke in 1957. In filling in as temporary president, Nixon was extremely careful, as he put it, "to absorb some of the duties of the President, and yet not to appear to be stepping into his shoes."

With Nixon out of Congress, a new anti-Communist spokesman

had taken his place. This was Senator Joseph McCarthy of Wisconsin, who was much louder in his accusations of Communists in American government than Nixon had ever been. McCarthy claimed that the Eisenhower administration, and especially the State Department, was filled with long-term Communists. Ike tried to avoid a direct confrontation with McCarthy, using Nixon as a go-between to deal with the Wisconsin senator. This technique worked all right for a time, but eventually the Eisenhower administration had to break with McCarthy, whose accusations became more and more irresponsible. Eventually most of McCarthy's claims were proved to be without merit, although a number of reputations were irreparably damaged by these false accusations. Finally the Wisconsin senator was censured by the Senate for his actions, and he dropped from sight as a legitimate critic of the administration.

Having faithfully fulfilled his duties as second in command to the nation's chief executive, Nixon was rewarded with the Republican party's nomination for president in 1960. His running mate was Henry Cabot Lodge, Jr., United Nations ambassador. Nixon and Lodge's Democrat opponents were John F. Kennedy of Massachusetts and Senator Lyndon Baines Johnson of Texas.

The highlights of the Nixon-Kennedy presidential race were four television debates between the two top candidates, the first such debates in history. They were also broadcast by radio, and interestingly, the majority of radio listeners thought Nixon was the debate winner. But those who watched the debates on TV—and this seemed to be the majority of those who voted that fall—were certain the youthful Kennedy had won. Whether it was due to poor cosmetic makeup or due simply to the fact that Nixon was not as photogenic as Kennedy, the viewing audience responded more positively to the charismatic Kennedy. Afterwards, Nixon reported that his mother had telephoned him from California to ask if he were ill. The nation had now had its first experience with the crucial importance of a favorable TV image in the electoral process.

But the election itself was a virtual tie. Kennedy did finally win—by a slim 100,000 votes—although there were rumors of vote fraud in Texas and Illinois. Nixon, however, refused to contest the election.

This was the first election Nixon had ever lost. He then maintained a low political profile for two years, after which he ran for governor of California. This time he was defeated by the incumbent governor, Edmund G. "Pat" Brown, whose pro-American, anti-Communist slate was as clean as Nixon's. Following his defeat Nixon held what he referred to as his "last press conference." He used the occasion to denounce various members of the media, telling them along the way, "Well, you won't have Richard Nixon to kick around any more."

Nixon did appear to be definitely out of politics, at least as a candidate for any office. He did, however, support the Republican presidential nominee, Senator Barry Goldwater of Arizona, campaigning for him in some thirty-six states. With Goldwater's landslide defeat by Lyndon Johnson, the Republicans as a political party seemed to be in total disarray, and Nixon's future political chances appeared to be less than zero.

During this low period in his political life, Nixon had returned to the practice of law, first in his native California and then in New York City with a prestigious firm. There was little doubt that this change in scene was made by Nixon mainly to escape his image as a "loser." He also set about trying to bind up the wounds of the Republican party by raising millions of dollars in campaign funds and actively campaigning for Republican congressional candidates. By the time the 1968 presidential campaign got under way, Nixon's image as a possible presidential candidate had been rehabilitated.

As Nixon prepared to reenter the political arena, an important new factor had to be included in campaign strategy. This was the war in Vietnam in which the United States was involved and which was dividing the nation.

Nixon had strongly favored U.S. involvement in Vietnam since the mid-1950s. That was when the French had been driven out of the country by Ho Chi Minh and his Communist forces. Before World War II France had controlled Vietnam as part of colonial French Indochina. After World War II the Vietnamese wanted their independence, but the French wanted to recolonize the country. When they failed in this attempt, Vietnam was divided into north and south Vietnam with Ho Chi Minh and his Communist forces controlling the northern part of the country and the United States supporting what was hoped would be a democratic part, the Republic of South Vietnam.

The reason the United States got involved in this conflict was to prevent the spread of Communism from North Vietnam throughout Southeast Asia. This was called the domino theory: if one country fell to Communism, so the theory went, all of the neighboring countries would also fall. Nixon was a devout believer in the domino theory and had even tried to persuade President Eisenhower to go to the aid of the French, using nuclear weapons if necessary, to prevent their being driven out of the country. But Ike's stout military background had convinced him that the United States should not become involved in a land war on the Asian continent. He was also anti-Communist, however, and had favored U.S. aid to the Republic of South Vietnam when the country was divided.

Since Ike's modest involvement of the United States in Vietnam, the situation had developed into a major war there, and successive U.S. presidents—John Kennedy and Lyndon Johnson—had taken the United States deeper and deeper into the conflict. Meanwhile, on the home front there had been steadily increasing opposition to U.S. continued participation in the Vietnam War. This debate between the pro- and anti-Vietnam War segments of the voting public promised to play a major role in the 1968 presidential election and in the selection of the presidential nominees themselves.

The Democratic party virtually had to renominate Lyndon Johnson for a second term since he was the incumbent president, and a failure to do so would be a tacit admission of failure in national foreign policy. But Johnson was a hawk who had backed the war to the hilt, and there were peace-seeking doves in the party who wanted the war to end and who promised to end it if they were elected.

Most prominent among the Democratic doves was Senator Robert Kennedy of New York, brother of the late president, whose assassination had resulted in Johnson's becoming president. Another well-known and popular Democratic dove was Senator Eugene McCarthy, of Minnesota, who campaigned openly as a peace candidate.

By this time President Johnson was both war-weary and tired of being harshly criticized by the antiwar public. (Demonstrators outside the White House taunted Johnson by chanting, "LBJ, LBJ, How Many Kids Did You Kill Today?") In March of 1968 he announced that he would not be a candidate for reelection. This political bombshell not only encouraged the Bobby Kennedy backers, but it also revived hopes among the Republicans in general and Nixon in particular that the upcoming election might be theirs.

Then tragedy struck. While campaigning in California for the Democratic nomination, Robert Kennedy was shot and killed by Sirhan Sirhan, a Jordanian citizen who apparently committed the act in protest over the fact that Jordanians had no homeland. After Kennedy's assassination it seemed possible that McCarthy might get the Democratic presidential nomination, but it eventually went to Hubert Humphrey, who had served as Johnson's vice president. Outgoing President Johnson supported Humphrey's candidacy, but it was questionable whether this support was a help or hindrance since it colored Humphrey with the war paint of the Johnson administration.

The tragedy and the political civil war among the Democrats definitely aided the Republican comeback. Nixon proved he was still a vote-getter by competing and winning several important primary battles in New England and the Pacific Northwest. The men he defeated in these primaries were national figures, Governor George Romney of Michigan and Governor Nelson Rockefeller of New York. Nixon's victory over them sent him to the Republican National Convention in Miami as the clear favorite for the party's nomination.

And a favorite Nixon remained, receiving the presidential nomination on the first ballot. As his vice presidential running mate Nixon chose a virtual unknown, Governor Spiro Agnew of Maryland.

Actually the Vietnam War never really became an out-and-out campaign issue. Nixon adroitly accomplished this result by announcing early in the campaign against Humphrey that he would not comment on the war because he did not want to disrupt peace meetings that were then going on between the United States and Vietnamese representatives in Paris. This arrangement was, of course, agreeable to Humphrey and his campaign managers since they did not want to have to account for the wartime policies of the Democrats up to this point. Doubtless recalling the TV debate debacle with John Kennedy, Nixon this time ducked any debates with Humphrey.

On election day, November 5, 1968, Nixon became the nation's thirty-seventh president, defeating Hubert Humphrey 301 to 191 electoral votes. Forty-six electoral votes were won by third-party candidate George C. Wallace, a former governor of Alabama. Wallace was the American Independent party's candidate, but he did little except drain votes away from Nixon in the Deep South. Wallace was a racist candidate running in protest against recent federal civil rights legislation for blacks.

Nixon had now been out of political office for eight years, and at age fifty-six he was delighted to be back in harness.

6

The Nixon Administration

When Richard Milhous Nixon took over as thirty-seventh president of the United States on January 20, 1969, he named only one cabinet member who would later cause him difficulty. This was John N. Mitchell, who was appointed attorney general. But Nixon did bring with him into office several administrative aides and assistants who would play key roles in the disgrace of his administration.

H. R. "Bob" Haldeman—the initials stood for Harry Robbins— was Nixon's chief of staff. During the election campaign Haldeman had been Nixon's advance man and personal manager, and he had made it an ironclad rule that anyone who wanted to see Nixon had to see Haldeman first. This rule became holy writ in the White House.

Bob Haldeman had graduated from the University of California at Los Angeles in 1945. A year later he joined the West Coast office of the J. Walter Thompson advertising firm, where he soon became an account executive. But from 1956 on, he took a leave of absence from his advertising job to campaign for Richard Nixon every time Nixon ran for office. In 1968 Haldeman permanently left the J. Walter Thompson agency, even though he was now the West Coast office manager and a vice president, to work with Nixon on his presidential campaign.

Haldeman and Nixon shared several qualities. One was a capacity for endless work. Another was ruthlessness in fighting against any form of opposition. Each came from a strict religious background, Nixon having been reared in the Quaker faith, while Haldeman had been brought up as a Christian Scientist. Haldeman, however, still practiced his faith, neither smoking nor drinking and frowning upon those who did. Mrs. Nixon, in fact, who was fond of an occasional martini, once told the wife of an eastern governor whom the Nixons were visiting, "You know—I don't dare take a drink when Bob Haldeman's around." The president himself, who liked to drink and occasionally drank to excess, apparently ignored his chief of staff's opinions on this subject—if, indeed, any opinions were offered.

One of the first men asked by Haldeman to join the Nixon team was John Ehrlichman. Ehrlichman was now a lawyer in Seattle, Washington, but he and Haldeman had been fellow students at UCLA. There they had been active in campus politics, and Ehrlichman had worked in earlier Nixon campaigns. Like Haldeman, Ehrlichman was a devout Christian Scientist who neither smoked nor drank. He too was a workhorse and often put in sixteen hours a day at his job despite the fact that such a regimen kept him from his wife and their five children.

From his background Ehrlichman could easily be regarded as the all-American boy—an Eagle Scout in his youth and the lead navigator on twenty-six heavy bomber missions over Germany during World War II for which he was awarded several air medals and the Distinguished Flying Cross. Beneath his affable, hail-fellow-well-met exterior, however, was a will of iron and a ruthlessness that was equal to if not greater than that of Nixon and Haldeman.

Two young men from the J. Walter Thompson ad agency, Ronald Ziegler and Dwight Chapin, also joined the Nixon team thanks to invitations from Haldeman. Both would figure in the events that lay ahead. Herbert Klein, a California newspaperman, was Nixon's initial press adviser, but it was Ziegler who ended up as Nixon's press secretary.

Soon to be added to the Nixon team in the White House were

several other ambitious young men. These were John Dean, Charles Colson, and Jeb Magruder. Dean, just thirty-one, was a graduate of Ohio's Wooster College and the Georgetown Law School. Dean started out working for Attorney General John Mitchell but then became the president's chief counsel.

Colson, thirty-eight, a graduate of Brown University, came from Boston, where he had had a considerable amount of experience in hard-knuckle city and state politics. He had, in fact, something of a reputation as a bully. He also was known for his ability to get the job done no matter what its nature or the methods needed to accomplish it. Colson, like Dean, was a lawyer and a successful one. He joined the Nixon team at something of a financial sacrifice but indicated he intended to soon regain a sound financial condition under Nixon. An ex-Marine, Colson was aggressive in all of his relationships, including his dealings with the president. He was without scruples and indicated as much by attempting to muscle in between Nixon and Herb Klein and take over as main public relations man for the administration. Since Haldeman regarded Klein as a weak link with Nixon's political past, Colson soon had an inside track in the White House.

Magruder was also from the East Coast. He had attended public high school on Staten Island, New York, and then Williams College. There he had majored in political science and studied ethics under the Reverend William Sloane Coffin, who later moved to Yale, where he became a leading anti-Vietnam War spokesman. Magruder's course in ethics apparently did not rub off on him, for he was anything but ethical when Haldeman hired him and put him to work in Herb Klein's office as a "coordinator." Actually he served as an informant to keep Haldeman apprized of Klein's activities and to cooperate with Colson in becoming chief of public relations.

As the Nixon administration gradually moved forward in taking over the nation's government, some key figures were added and some removed from the Nixon team. There was also a key woman—Rose Mary Woods, Nixon's trusted and faithful secretary since 1951 when he had been vice president. She had known Nixon, however, since he was a congressman in 1947 and admired his work habits and frugality in handling public funds. Rose Mary Woods's loyalty was to be severely tested by the events of the next months, but she never wavered in her loyalties to President Nixon.

Nixon had come into office with what he said was a secret plan to end the war in Vietnam. If he had such a plan, it remained secret. What was divulged was Nixon's program of secretly bombing Cambodia (today's Kampuchea). When *The New York Times* broke this story, Nixon claimed that the reason for the bombing was that the North Vietnamese were using Cambodia as a sanctuary for their combat troops before and after battles with the United States and South Vietnamese forces.

The reaction against the Cambodian bombings escalated the anti-Vietnam War demonstrations in the United States, which were already at a fever pitch. The *Times'* disclosures infuriated Nixon and his team to such a degree that they began to place wiretaps in the homes and offices of State Department officials, members of the National Security Council, newspaper and television reporters, columnists, and correspondents.

This probably illegal "bugging" operation—it is illegal to put a wiretap on the phone of a private citizen without a court order—was done to find out who had leaked the classified information to the *Times*. The purpose also was to deter future leaks. The operations had been developed by John Ehrlichman, who had begun creating a private intelligence system for the president soon after entering the White House. His initial aides in this endeavor were two former members of the New York City Police Department's Bureau of Special Services, Jack Caulfield and Tony Ulasewicz. This original political espionage effort did little but stir resentment among members of the news media, but it did give powerful indication of future White House activities.

Although Nixon did escalate the war by his attacks on Cambodia, he did live up to another campaign promise to reduce American participation in the war by beginning to bring U.S. troops home. In July 1969, 25,000 troops were returned from Vietnam. This program continued until by the fall of 1972 the American military strength in Vietnam had been reduced from just over half a million men to 32,000.

In the midst of Nixon's efforts to end the war, his administration was struck a blow by the publication of the so-called "Pentagon Papers" in the spring of 1971.

The Pentagon is the five-sided building in Washington housing the U.S. Department of Defense. During the Lyndon Johnson administration, Secretary of Defense Robert S. McNamara had a report prepared that gave a detailed account of U.S. involvement in the Vietnam War. One of the people who prepared this report was a young man named Daniel Ellsberg.

At the beginning of the war Ellsberg was a "hawk," one who strongly favored American participation in the conflict. As he worked on the report, however, Ellsberg gradually switched to an anti-Vietnam War position. As a newborn "dove" of peace, Ellsberg thought all U.S. citizens should see his report. But the Pentagon Papers were classified as secret. Nevertheless, Ellsberg soon began to leak them to the press. They were first published in *The New York Times* in June of 1971 and then elsewhere. The Nixon administration tried to prevent their being published, but the courts ruled against such prior censorship.

What the Pentagon Papers disclosed was that a major portion of the war had been carried on secretly so that the American public and even the U.S. Congress had not been fully informed of government activities. Nixon and his aides agreed that it was important to try and discredit Daniel Ellsberg. If he were not discredited, he might continue to disclose secret information that could irreparably damage the presidency. Some months later Ellsberg was brought to trial for disclosing secret information, but he was acquitted.

Before Ellsberg was tried, the president urged both Haldeman and Ehrlichman to take some sort of action against him. In response to Nixon's urging, a so-called "Plumbers' Unit" was formed to stop all future information leaks to the press. The number one priority, however, was "to find out all that could be found out about Mr. Ellsberg's associations and his motives." The priority was in President Nixon's words.

To head up the Plumbers' Unit, Ehrlichman chose Egil Krogh, a former member of Ehrlichman's Seattle law firm. Krogh had worked for the Nixon administration as a liaison man with the FBI, but Ehrlichman wanted the Plumbers' Unit to work independently from the FBI, which the Nixon team did not wholly trust. Krogh, in turn, recruited E. Howard Hunt, who had worked unsuccessfully for the CIA, and G. Gordon Liddy, formerly with the FBI, who was also experienced in covert operations while working on narcotics control with the Treasury Department. A third original plumber was David Young, who had been a member of Henry Kissinger's national security staff.

As the 1972 national elections approached, Nixon established a campaign organization named the Committee to Reelect the President, CRP, but generally referred to as CREEP. CREEP collected more than $60 million for use in the campaign, much of it gathered illegally and used for illegal purposes.

Heading up CREEP originally was Jeb Magruder as deputy director. He was never considered aggressive enough in this role, however, and was replaced by former Attorney General John Mitchell. Magruder, at an increase in salary, was kicked upstairs, where he helped operate a so-called "Dirty Tricks" campaign along with Dwight Chapin and Donald Segretti. Dirty Tricks operations consisted of everything from placing spies in the opposition's camp to making false phone calls to cancel opponents' speaking engagements or other programmed events. Once several hundred pizzas were ordered to be delivered to an unsuspecting Democratic meeting of top officials.

Overall campaign intelligence operations were now placed in the hands of John Dean. Dean pushed hard to include G. Gordon Liddy and E. Howard Hunt as the heads of any new Plumbers' Unit, and the two were approved for renewed espionage activity by Haldeman, Ehrlichman, and Mitchell. Such activity was not long in coming.

On the early morning (2:30 A.M.) of June 17, 1972, a security guard, Frank Wills, found a door latch taped open at the Watergate complex in Washington, D.C. Wills immediately called police, who caught five members of CREEP burglarizing the Democratic National Committee's headquarters. The five men were Bernard L. Barker, Virgilio R. Gonzales, Eugenio R. Martinez, James McCord, Jr., and Frank A. Sturges. All five were wearing rubber gloves. One carried a walkie-talkie. Others carried numerous rolls of unexposed film, two cameras, lock picks, and bugging devices to be used on telephones or placed to pick up room conversations.

When the men were first apprehended, it was not known that they were working for CREEP, and no immediate connection was made between them and the White House. Several of the burglars apparently were Cubans who had been connected with the failed Bay of Pigs invasion of Cuba. This operation early in the Kennedy administration was aimed at overthrowing dictator Fidel Castro. Since then a number of Cubans involved in the abortive invasion had continued to work off and on for the U.S. government under the mistaken idea that whatever undercover job they were given to do was somehow tied in with a continued attempt to overthrow Castro. At least one of the burglars, James McCord, Jr., apparently also had CIA connections and had been the security chief of CREEP.

The names of G. Gordon Liddy and E. Howard Hunt were brought into the police investigation of the burglary when their names were found on scraps of paper in the pockets of two of the burglars. Since both of these men had connections as consultants to the administration, the White House was brought into the picture. Nevertheless, both CREEP chairman Mitchell and President Nixon vehemently denied any tie-in with the Watergate affair. Nixon, in fact, said: "I can say categorically that investigations indicate that no one in the White House staff, no one in this Administration, presently employed, was involved in this very bizarre incident." The president was lying. He had already begun to try and cover up White House involvement in the affair.

Since at this time President Nixon still had much credibility, the general public was inclined to lose interest in Watergate.

A short time after Nixon made his statement in late August of 1972, all five men, plus Liddy and Hunt, were indicted for burglary. Their trial, however, would not begin until January of 1973, some months after the presidential election.

But not everyone was forgetting about Watergate. Lawrence O'-Brien, the Democratic national chairman, was convinced the Republicans were behind the attempt to burglarize and bug his party's headquarters and publicly denounced the Nixon administration for its apparent role in the affair. And the reportorial staffs of several major newspapers, especially the *Washington Post, New York Times*, and *Los Angeles Times,* as well as news magazines such as *Time* and *Newsweek,* remained active in their investigation of the Watergate break-in. All of these media investigations centered on trying to link Watergate with the White House.

But public interest continued to remain on the elections and the possible end of the Vietnam War. Election interest peaked when the Democrats blundered in their first selection of a vice presidential nominee.

At their national convention in July at Miami Beach, the Democrats chose Senator George S. McGovern of South Dakota as their presidential candidate and Senator Thomas F. Eagleton of Missouri as their vice presidential candidate. Soon, however, the national media were featuring stories about the fact that Senator Eagleton had in the 1960s been hospitalized and taken shock treatments for "nervous exhaustion." As a result, Eagleton stepped down and was replaced by R. Sargent Shriver, Jr., former head of the Peace Corps under President Kennedy.

Nixon and Agnew were renominated by acclamation for second

terms at the Republican convention, also in Miami Beach, in August.

Because of the Eagleton fiasco and the fact that Nixon did seem to be winding down the Vietnam War, Nixon's reelection was generally conceded by political pundits. Nationwide polls also gave the incumbent president a comfortable lead. Nevertheless, Nixon and his White House team went about the reelection campaign as if the president were the underdog and stood a good chance of losing the 1972 election. They seemed bent on not merely defeating the opposition but destroying it.

In November Nixon and Agnew won in a landslide, administering to McGovern and Shriver the greatest political defeat of any Democratic presidential and vice presidential candidates in the country's history. Nixon won everywhere except in Massachusetts and the District of Columbia. The Republican candidates were reelected with 61 percent of the popular vote and 520 out of a possible 538 electoral votes.

Nixon's approval rating on the part of the public was further enhanced by the fact that National Security Adviser Henry Kissinger succeeded in Vietnam War peace negotiations early in 1973. On January 1 in Paris, Kissinger and North Vietnamese representative Le Duc Tho signed an agreement to end the war. Further negotiations would follow, but this agreement essentially ended the conflict. Nixon then ordered that the bombing of North Vietnam by the U.S. Air Force end on January 15, just five days before his inauguration to a second term.

Overwhelming public approval, however, had its disadvantages as well as advantages. Its major disadvantage was the fact that it seemed to breed an overconfidence in the members of the Nixon team that expressed itself in arrogance and disdain toward the other branches of government, both legislative and judicial. Nixon and his White House team had always acted as if they were the only important heads of American government. Now they tried secretly to defy Congress and the Department of Justice by a continued cover-up of the Watergate affair.

Early in 1973 the five men caught at Watergate, plus Liddy and Hunt, went on trial for burglary and breaking the anti-bugging law. Hunt and four of the other plumbers immediately pleaded guilty. Liddy and Mc-Cord then stood trial and were found guilty ninety minutes after the trial ended on January 30. None of the plumbers would tell what they knew about the Watergate affair, and several newspapers and news magazines claimed the burglars were being paid to keep quiet.

Finally on March 23 the burglars were brought up before Judge John J. Sirica for sentencing. The judge had delayed passing sentence in hopes that one or more of the guilty men would talk in return for a suspended sentence. On the day of sentencing, McCord told Judge Sirica that he would tell what he knew. Several days later McCord testified to a newly formed Senate Watergate investigating committee that John Mitchell, now at CREEP but attorney general at the time of the break-in, had been in overall charge of the plumbers from the beginning and that CREEP funds had since been used to pay off the burglars in return for their silence. Mitchell admitted that CREEP funds had been used but only to defend the burglars.

Among the prison sentences meted out to the five Watergate burglars were jail terms from thirteen to fifteen months. Liddy, who refused to cooperate with authorities, eventually served fifty-two months. Hunt served thirty-three months.

The Senate Watergate investigating committee with Senator Sam Ervin, Jr., of North Carolina in charge had been established early in February. This committee, along with the Washington grand jury and national news media, was now engaged in investigating all aspects of the Watergate affair. The first major discovery of the Senate committee was the fact that the president had been taping all conversations in his office. These tapes, Senator Ervin and his colleagues suspected, might answer the insistent query of Senator Howard Baker of Tennessee "What did the President know, and when did he know it?"

Alexander Butterfield was another UCLA friend of Bob Haldeman's who had been invited to work in the White House soon after Nixon took office. Butterfield—who had no part in the Watergate affair—was a personable young man who made a point of maintaining a low profile as Haldeman's top aide. Nevertheless, when the Ervin Committee began to investigate the possible role of White House officials in the Watergate affair, one of the first men they quizzed was Butterfield. Interviews with Haldeman had gotten Ervin Committee staff members Scott Armstrong and Don Sanders nowhere. Perhaps they would be more successful with Haldeman's deputy.

It took several hours of quizzing Butterfield in the new Senate office building, but finally Armstrong and Sanders hit pay dirt. The date was July 13, 1973.

The investigators were not wholly satisfied with Butterfield's responses to questions about how notes were taken and records kept of meetings in the Oval Office. Finally Butterfield was asked if there were tape recordings made of the meetings.

"I was hoping you fellows wouldn't ask me that," Butterfield replied. Yes, it turned out, there were tape recordings. In fact, all conversations in the Oval Office had been taped for months.

While the investigators were startled at Butterfield's reply, most congressmen and other Washington officials knew that White House tape recordings were not especially new. As far back as President Franklin D. Roosevelt's day, there had been a primitive tape recording device in the chief executive's office. Presidents Kennedy and Johnson also taped some of their conversations. None of these devices, however, approached the voice-activated sophistication of the Nixon recording apparatus, which was designed to record every word uttered in the room. All earlier devices had been simple, hand-operated recorders that missed as much conversation as they recorded.

Butterfield testified about the "listening devices" in the Oval Office before the Ervin Committee on the afternoon of July 13. His testimony, like most of the congressional testimony, was shown on national television. It lasted only fifteen minutes, but the nationwide stir it caused finally resulted in Senator Sam Ervin's asking President

Nixon for some of the tapes of the president's conversations made at about the time of the Watergate burglary. The president rejected the request on the grounds of executive privilege. Finally, however, the U.S. Supreme Court ordered the president to turn over the tapes to the Senate committee. Reluctantly and with numerous delays Nixon ultimately did so.

Meanwhile, several other key members of the Nixon team were testifying before the Ervin Committee. Among them were Ehrlichman, Dean, Mitchell, Haldeman, Magruder, Colson, and several other lesser lights. The hearings involving this testimony went on for many weeks.

In the early days of the Ervin Committee another blow struck the White House, one that had nothing to do with the Watergate scandal. In August of 1973 there were widespread media reports that Vice President Spiro Agnew was being investigated by U.S. attorneys in Baltimore for accepting bribes while he was the governor of Maryland and before he had become vice president.

Agnew, of course, denied all criminal charges, calling them "damned lies." Nevertheless, the investigation continued, and suddenly on October 10, 1973, Agnew announced his resignation as vice president. He pleaded no contest to one charge of evading income taxes on the alleged bribes. After the government presented evidence that Agnew had accepted more than $100,000 from construction firms to obtain Maryland state contracts, Agnew was placed on three years' probation and fined $10,000. Despite his "nolo contendere" plea to the bribe charges, a plea that was a virtual admission of guilt, the former vice president continued to profess his innocence.

Immediately after Agnew's resignation, President Nixon, under the recently passed Twenty-fifth Amendment to the Constitution, nominated Gerald R. Ford, Republican congressman from Michigan, as the nation's fortieth vice president. He was sworn in on December 6, 1973.

As the month-long testimony before Congress of the various White House officials continued, it became clear that President Nixon would have little choice but to fire most of the members of his team. The president himself had not yet been shown as having been involved in either the planning of Watergate or its cover-up, but certainly many of his aides had been clearly implicated.

Eventually it was proved that some twenty-five persons involved in the Watergate affair were guilty enough to be sent to jail. The maximum amount of time served was fifty-two months. Former Attorney General and CREEP Director John Mitchell was convicted of conspiracy, obstruction of justice, and lying under oath to cover up the break-in. He served nineteen months.

Haldeman served eighteen months for conspiracy, perjury, and obstruction of justice. Ehrlichman, convicted of these same counts plus planning the raid on Ellsberg's psychiatrist's office, also served eighteen months and had his license to practice law suspended.

Dean, because of his cooperation with the prosecutors, served only four months for conspiracy. He was actually the first among Nixon's inner circle of aides to actually testify against the members of the Nixon team involved in Watergate.

Interestingly, most of the main figures in Watergate later wrote books about the affair from which several made hundreds of thousands of dollars.

When the tapes were turned over the the Ervin Committee, one tape, it was discovered contained an 18-1/2 minute gap. Those 18-1/2 minutes, experts agreed, had been purposely erased. In testimony before Congress, Nixon's faithful secretary, Rose Mary Woods, tried to demonstrate how those 18-1/2 minutes might have been accidentally erased by misuse of a foot control pedal. This demonstration, however, was never wholly convincing.

The gap in this one tape did bring up one other question: "Why didn't President Nixon simply destroy all of the tapes? There was never any adequate answer to this question, although it was suggested that Nixon thought future historians would somehow find enough information on them to partially exonerate him.

This possibility seemed remote when a damning and clearly impeachable piece of evidence finally turned up on an early tape. On it President Nixon plainly indicated he wanted the Watergate break-in, or "plan" as he called it, covered up. "I don't give a ————what happens," the president could be heard insisting, "I want you to stonewall it. Let them plead the Fifth Amendment, cover-up, or anything else if it'll save it, save the plan." Most damning evidence on the tape was Nixon's instructions to Haldeman that, if necessary, Haldeman should obstruct the FBI's investigation of the break-in.

Haldeman: "And you seem to think the thing to do is to get the FBI to stop?"

Nixon: "Right. Fine."

Haldeman: ". . . and the proposal would be that Ehrlichman and I call them in and say, ah ————."

Nixon: "All right, fine. . . . Play it tough. That's the way they play it, and that's the way we are going to play it."

With most of his aides fired, Nixon became a lonelier and lonelier man in the White House. And when the tape was discovered that disclosed his own involvement in the cover-up, it became clear to numerous Nixon friends and government officials that Nixon himself would probably have to go.

On June 6, 1974, the Watergate grand jury that had indicted most of the twenty-five persons involved in the scandal named the president as an unindicted coconspirator in the cover-up. The House of Representatives Judiciary Committee that was now considering impeachment proceedings against Nixon received the damning information from the Watergate grand jury and added it to the evidence it was collecting.

Soon after this blow Richard G. Kleindienst, who had succeeded Mitchell as attorney general, received a suspended sentence for misleading the Senate investigating committee. Kleindienst's sentencing marked the first time a cabinet officer had been convicted of a felony since the Teapot Dome scandal of the Harding administration.

The House Judiciary Committee, headed by Representative Peter Rodino of New Jersey, then began a public debate on whether or not to impeach the president. The committee subsequently voted for Nixon's impeachment on the grounds of obstructing justice in the Watergate cover-up, plus abuse of power and violating his presidential oath of office.

"Richard M. Nixon," the committee report concluded, "has acted in a manner contrary to his trust as president and subversive of constitutional government, to the great prejudice of the cause of law and justice and to the manifest injury of the people of the United States. Wherefore, Richard M. Nixon, by such conduct, warrants impeachment and trial, and removal from office."

Facing almost certain impeachment when the whole House voted on its committee's report, Nixon was urged by key members of his own Republican party, as well as opposition Democrats, to resign. Late in July Nixon spent a few days with his speech writers at the Camp David presidential retreat in Maryland. He then returned to Washington and on the evening of August 8, 1974, delivered a nationally televised speech in which he announced his proposed resignation from the presidency to be effective the next day at noon. Nowhere in this speech did he admit his guilt, stating only that "it had become evident to me that I no longer have a strong enough political base in Congress to remain in office."

On August 9, 1974, Vice President Gerald Ford took over as president. One month later President Ford granted former President Nixon a "full, free, and absolute pardon" for all offenses committed during his administration.

Section Four

The Reagan Administration's
Iran-Contra Scandal

Ronald W. Reagan

7

Ronald W. Reagan:
From Sports Broadcaster and
Actor to President

Ronald Reagan's life itself was something like one of the many romantic movies in which he acted before becoming governor of California and then president of the United States. Born poor, he eventually became a rich man and the head of one of the most powerful nations in the world. Like most movies, however, there were some villains as well as heroes in the script of Ronald Reagan's life. The villains almost prevailed during the hero's second term as president. But again, as in the movies, in the end the hero, Ronald Reagan, managed to win through and provide a happy ending.

Ronald Wilson Reagan was born on February 6, 1911, at Tampico, Illinois. He was the younger of two children, both boys, born to John and Nellie (Wilson) Reagan. Ronald's older brother, Neil, was born in 1909 and had a boyhood nickname of "Moon." Moon called his younger brother "Dutch" because he thought Ronald was a sissy name. The future president was called Dutch Reagan by family and friends during most of his early life, including his stint as a radio sports announcer.

President Reagan was prone to romanticize his turn-of-the-century boyhood in several Illinois small towns as a kind of Huck

Finn-Tom Sawyer idyll. The truth of the matter was the Reagan family life was one of severe poverty and probably not nearly so romantic as Reagan later remembered it. His father was an unsuccessful shoe salesman, and the family was held together by Nellie Reagan, who worked in a dress shop and at similar jobs for less than twenty dollars a week.

After an itinerant life in various central and southern Illinois towns—the family also lived briefly in Chicago—the Reagans finally settled down long enough in Dixon for the boys to go to high school. Neil was physically larger than Ronald and was able to compete successfully and easily in sports. Despite his short height—five feet three inches—and light weight—110 pounds—Ronald went out for football both at Dixon High School and later in college, making up in fight, according to his brother, what he lacked in size. Later, of course, Ronald grew rapidly, standing over six feet tall as president and weighing about 185 pounds.

Reagan graduated from Dixon High School in 1928. The family still had no money, but Ronald was able to obtain a scholarship to attend nearby Eureka College, a small Disciples of Christ school. He also earned money washing dishes at a fraternity house and during summer vacations earned $18 a week as a lifeguard—excellent money during the economic depression years of the 1930s. As a lifeguard for some seven years, Reagan reputedly saved seventy-five or eighty lives, exactly how many depending upon who was telling the story.

At Eureka College Reagan became active in campus politics and performed for the first time as an actor. By now an extremely handsome and popular young man, he was also president of his class. As a member of the school drama club, Reagan had roles in several plays, and acting interested him so much that when he graduated from Eureka in 1932, he decided he would get a job as a radio actor. These were the pretelevision days, of course, but radio drama was extremely popular and employed many young actors.

However, Reagan's first radio job was as a sports announcer at station WOC in Davenport, Iowa, just across the Mississippi River from Dixon. His pay at WOC was $10 a game, but he proved to be a popular announcer and in a few months was hired by radio station WHO in Des Moines for $75 a week.

Dutch Reagan soon became WHO's most popular announcer. Not only did he broadcast many baseball games and other sporting events "live," but he also realistically reconstructed games from nothing more than telegraphed reports. These broadcasts consisted of Reagan sitting in a studio in Des Moines into which was fed taped telegraph reports of a game in progress in another city. From these brief telegraphed reports Reagan would "announce" the game as though he were actually witnessing the action. In the background he would have available various recordings of crowd noises and music and other sounds that he could turn on to increase the realism of the action.

Listeners always knew that the play-by-play reports of such broadcasts were actually being faked (among other things the telegraph ticker could be heard over the air), but they seemed to enjoy listening to the game in this fashion rather than hearing merely a bare bones report of the action. Reagan was just one of several announcers doing these faked broadcasts throughout the country, but his reconstructed reports of Chicago Cubs and St. Louis Cardinal games were always the most realistic. In later years Reagan enjoyed reminiscing about certain melodramatic moments in baseball games when he would announce that a pitch was on the way toward the batter just when the telegraph report broke down due to mechanical problems. In such instances, Reagan claimed, he ad-libbed foul balls and other time-killing action for several minutes until the telegraph ticker kicked in again.

In 1937 Reagan was in California covering the Chicago Cubs' spring training baseball games on Catalina Island for WHO. He had never gotten over being bitten by the acting bug, and he now got a colleague to arrange a screen test for him in Hollywood. The test was successful, and Reagan was hired by the Warner Brothers Studio at a salary of $200 a week. This was regarded as a princely amount at the time, but soon Reagan would be earning much more.

Starting out in small parts in so-called "B" movies, he eventually played leading roles in such popular "A" pictures successes as *King's Row, Knute Rockne—All American*, and some fifty other films. The Rockne movie gave Reagan what was perhaps his most famous line of dialogue. In it he played a young football player, George Gipp, who died prematurely. On his deathbed Gipp, according to the movie script, told Rockne (Pat O'Brien) that sometime in the future when Notre Dame's football team was in desperate need of a victory, Rockne should ask the players "to go out there and win one for the Gipper." Off and on during his presidency, Reagan resurrected this line, and it never failed to win great applause.

Reagan was a successful movie actor for some twenty years. During this period, on January 25, 1940, he married a successful young actress, Jane Wyman. They had two children, a daughter, Maureen, born in 1941, and a son, Michael, adopted in 1945.

Late in the year Maureen was born, the United States entered World War II. The following year Reagan joined the Army Air Corps, but he saw no combat duty. All during the war he remained in Hollywood making training films for Air Corps flyers. In later years Reagan was somewhat prone to exaggerate his wartime experiences, once telling a foreign official that he had helped film grim scenes at Nazi death camps when they were liberated by advancing Allied troops, but Captain Reagan's only filming was done in California. At war's end in 1945 he returned to acting as a civilian.

Early in the postwar period Reagan began to be seriously interested in politics. In 1947 he was elected president of the Screen Actors Guild. He served in this post until 1952 and then again from 1959 to 1960. As guild president he succeeded in getting medical insurance and pension improvements for guild members.

Up until this time Reagan had always been an ardent Franklin D. Roosevelt New Deal Democrat. Now, however, he began to be suspicious of the ultra-liberals and what he decided were Communists who were trying to take over not only the guild but also much of the rest of Hollywood's motion picture industry. More and more of Reagan's time became devoted to guild and state and national politics in an effort to rid the country of the Communist influence. As he became less interested in motion pictures, his wife became less and less interested in him and his political activities. Reagan and Jane Wyman were divorced in 1948. She went on to score successes in such films as *Johnny Belinda*, for which she was awarded an Oscar as best actress, and later in television dramas.

While Reagan was head of the Screen Actors Guild, he became acquainted with a young actress named Nancy Davis, who was also an active anti-Communist. They fell in love and were married on March 4, 1952. They had two children, Patricia, born in 1953, and Ronald, Jr., born in 1958. The Reagans worked together in only one film, *Hellcats of the Navy*, in 1957. After that Nancy Reagan retired to become a housewife, and her husband tried to carry on his acting career. For some reason, however, he was offered fewer and fewer motion picture roles.

He did, however, continue his crusade as a conservative spokesman and became a public relations after-dinner speaker for the General Electric Company. He also became the host of a television series sponsored by General Electric from 1954 to 1962. Then he hosted another TV series, *Death Valley Days*, in which he also occasionally acted.

In the 1960s Reagan switched from being a registered Democrat to a registered Republican. With his strong stand against big government, the California Republican party became interested in having him as one of their political spokesmen. When Barry Goldwater ran as the Republican nominee for U.S. president in 1964, Reagan gave a widely watched and widely reported TV speech in favor of Goldwater's candidacy. In it he beat the conservative drum for less government control and more individual freedom of choice and action. In response to the speech, hundreds of thousands of dollars in contributions poured into the Republican campaign chest. Goldwater lost the election, but many people, including important Republican politicians, remembered Reagan's ringing speech and decided there must be a place in California politics for him.

Reagan at first scoffed at all suggestions that he himself run for office. But in 1965 he was asked to run for governor of the state on the Republican ticket against the incumbent governor, Democrat Edmund G."Pat" Brown. Reagan decided to run and easily won the primary over the former mayor of San Francisco, George Christopher. But the race against Pat Brown in the general election promised to be another matter. Brown was seeking a third term in office and was thought to be unbeatable, especially by an ex-movie actor with no experience in public office. This was the same Pat Brown who had soundly defeated Nixon in the 1962 California gubernatorial race, and Nixon had had a much better political track record than Reagan.

But Reagan was convinced that California's voters were tired of old "pols" and politics as usual and that he could bring a refreshing change to the governorship. Rather than playing down his experience as an actor, Reagan played it up and prevailed upon a number of his actor colleagues to stump the state for him. Surprisingly, Reagan won by almost a million votes. A new national political candidate appeared to have arrived on the scene.

Reagan took office as California's new governor on January 2, 1967. In his campaign Reagan had promised to cut taxes and the cost of running the state. But he soon discovered that California was some $200 million in debt and new taxes were inevitable. Nevertheless, Reagan proved to be an extremely popular governor—he was elected to a second term in 1970—and by the time he left office, the state treasury showed a surplus of some $500 million.

Under Reagan, however, the California state payroll had grown by 40,000 new employees despite the fact that he had promised to cut it. He did cut back on welfare and relief spending, but he made these reductions simply by cutting off from the relief rolls thousands of needy people. The public consensus on the Reagan stewardship as governor, however, was that he left the state in better shape than he found it.

Reagan decided not to run for a third term as governor. By now he had his eye on the presidency. In 1968 Reagan had made an abortive bid to get the Republican presidential nomination by having his name entered in the Oregon primary. He was defeated there by Nixon. Nevertheless, Reagan announced his candidacy at the Republican national convention. Nixon won the nomination on the first ballot, and Reagan and his backers then decided they would try again in 1976.

After leaving the governorship Reagan retired to his 700-acre ranch near Santa Barbara. He was now independently wealthy, having made astute real estate investments on his early Hollywood earnings. He continued to earn money from speaking engagements and also had both moral and financial support from a number of affluent California businessmen who saw in Reagan their future conservative champion in the White House.

By 1976 Reagan's opponent for the Republican nomination for president was Gerald Ford, who had succeeded Nixon as president when Nixon resigned after the Watergate scandal. Reagan and Ford ran an extremely close race for the nomination, but at the Republican National Convention in Kansas City, Missouri, on August 19, Ford was the winner by the narrow margin of 1,187 votes to 1,070. The Republicans had not refused the presidential nomination to an incumbent chief executive since 1884 when James G. Blaine was chosen over President Chester A. Arthur.

Again Reagan retired to his California ranch, where he would have to wait another four years for a chance to become president. Meanwhile, Georgia peanut farmer and staunch Democrat Jimmy Carter defeated Ford in the 1976 presidential race, so Reagan, if he indeed decided to run again in 1980, would have not only an incumbent president to defeat but a leader of the opposite party. There were those who thought this might be an easier job than running against a member of his own party as had been the case in the Reagan-Ford nomination contest.

There were also those who thought Reagan might be getting too old to seek national office—after all he would be almost seventy in 1980—but Reagan and his backers didn't think so. Reagan had retained most of the youthful good looks that had helped make him a movie star. He was also physically vigorous and his hair remained the same dark chestnut color it had always been. Some observers insisted that Reagan dyed his hair, but this was stoutly denied by his aides, his barber, and his wife Nancy.

Reagan formally announced that he would run against the incumbent president, Jimmy Carter, on November 13, 1979. He was not alone, however. More than half a dozen other Republicans also announced they too would run. In the Democratic camp Senator Edward Kennedy of Massachusetts, younger brother of the late President John Kennedy, looked like a formidable opponent if he were able to wrest the nomination from Carter.

Reagan's most serious competition for the Republican nomination came from George Bush, an oil millionaire and former congressman from Texas. He was also a former director of the Central Intelligence Agency (CIA). Bush, in fact, defeated Reagan in the early Iowa caucuses (something like primaries in other states) in January of 1980. But Reagan managed to recover in the following primary in New Hampshire, defeating not only Bush but all of his other Republican opponents as well. He then went on to win a majority of the remaining primaries.

The Republicans held their national convention in Detroit on July 16. Reagan was nominated by an overwhelming margin on the first ballot. He then chose Bush as his vice presidential running mate.

A month later the Democrats held their convention in New York City. Edward Kennedy had defeated Carter in primaries in several major states, but Carter finally won the nomination for his second term in office by a two-to-one margin.

Much of the Reagan-Carter election battle centered around a difficult international situation that had developed between the United States and the country of Iran during the last year of Carter's term as president. Iranian Islamic revolutionaries had overthrown the Iranian government late in 1979, driving out of the country its longtime leader, Muhammad Reza Shah Pahlevi. The Shah had been a close ally of the United States ever since the United States, through the CIA, had helped the Shah come to power in 1953. The revolutionaries consequently were not only enemies of the Shah but also enemies of the United States. In fact, the Iranian Islamic leader of the revolutionaries, the Ayatollah Ruhollah Khomeini, referred to the United States as "the Great Satan." As a result of this enmity, late in 1979 Iranian fanatics stormed the U.S. embassy in the Iranian capital of Tehran, taking captive some fifty-two American citizens and holding them as hostages.

The Carter administration had done virtually everything in its power to get these hostages released—including an abortive helicopter rescue mission—but nothing had been successful. In the end these hostages would be held for 444 days and would not be released until the beginning of the Reagan presidency.

The unfortunate Iranian situation, plus worsening economic conditions within the United States—both inflation and interest rates had soared under Carter—were too much of a handicap for the incumbent president to overcome. While it was expected that the race between Reagan and Carter would be a close one, on election day November 4, 1980, Reagan won in all except six states and the District of Columbia. His landslide victory gave him 489 electoral votes to 49 for Carter.

8

The Reagan Administration

Ronald Wilson Reagan was sworn into office as the nation's fortieth president on January 20, 1981. He was the first actor to become president and also the oldest man to become the nation's chief executive. Sixty-nine when he was elected, he turned seventy less than a month after he took office.

The Reagan administration began auspiciously. Right at the end of his inaugural address President Reagan announced that the fifty-two hostages that had been held by Iran for more than a year were being freed. Later there were rumors that for political purposes Reagan aides had worked out a deal with Iran not to free the hostages until Reagan became president. These rumors, however, were never confirmed, and Reagan gave full credit to ex-President Carter and the State Department for obtaining release of the hostages in exchange for returning to Iran some $8 billion in funds frozen in American banks. As a gesture of American foreign policy unity, President Reagan arranged for Carter to fly to Germany, the first stop on the hostages' way home, to greet them.

But the Reagan administration almost ended in stark tragedy while it was just beginning. On March 30, 1981, an attempt to assassinate the recently inaugurated president was made outside a Washington,

D.C., hotel. The would-be assassin was twenty-five-year-old John W. Hinckley, Jr., a mentally disturbed young man who fired six shots from a revolver. One of the shots hit President Reagan on his left side. Other shots hit Reagan's press secretary, a Secret Service agent, and a policeman. Reagan was rushed to a hospital, where he was successfully operated on, and he recovered in a few weeks. Hinckley was captured at the scene of his crime and later committed to a mental hospital.

Most of President Reagan's cabinet members and aides had backgrounds in big business rather than in academic circles or the government itself. While this had its positive side in that these ex-businessmen and women were excellent administrators who were used to acting on their own and getting a job accomplished, it also had its negative side. There was an apparent lack of ethical scruples in just how things got done, with not sufficient attention being paid to the fine points of either legality or constitutionality.

As James MacGregor Burns, a noted presidential historian, has pointed out, "Big business [is] a world [that is] not necessarily corrupt but one where they are operating under the rules of business. And they draw people who often are free enterprisers, individualists, people who accept the notion that one has to climb up the greasy ladder and don't have to worry about the rules so much to do it."

President Reagan was not the type of top administrator to maintain tight control over those who worked for him. He was, in fact, inclined to give them almost a completely free rein, too much free rein some critics said, in handling their part of the nation's affairs. What resulted was widespread wrongdoing and even political corruption.

By the time of President Reagan's second term in office, the U.S. Justice Department reported that some seven special counsels had been appointed to investigate charges of wrongdoing among administration officials. Two of these counsels were charged with looking into the activities of the head of the Justice Department, Attorney General Edwin Meese.

Charges against government officials included abuse of power in carrying out foreign policies, presidential associates helping friends get government contracts, and government aides making private profits from their government service. In all, according to the House of Representatives' Subcommittee on Civil Service, more than 225 Reagan aides allegedly were guilty of ethical or criminal wrongdoing. Not all of these alleged offenses were major in nature and not all of those accused were found guilty. But the sheer number involved indicated an ethically flawed atmosphere during the Reagan administration.

The tone of the Reagan administration was perhaps established during the first election campaign in 1980 when someone in the Reagan camp apparently stole a notebook containing all of the notes made by Reagan's opponent, Jimmy Carter, for the scheduled debates between Carter and Reagan. Although Reagan's aides denied the theft, Reagan did not hesitate to use the material contained in the notebook.

Soon after the Reagan administration began, National Security Adviser Richard Allen resigned after accepting $1,000 for arranging an interview between Nancy Reagan and Japanese journalists. Questionable stock dealings resulted in the resignations of Max Hugel of the CIA and Thomas C. Reed, White House national security counselor.

Interior Secretary James Watt resigned for purely ethical reasons, although he was earlier accused of using government funds to pay for private parties. His resignation followed his crass comment about a new Interior Department commission that he said included, "Three Democrats, two Republicans, every kind of mix you can have. I have a black, a woman, two Jews, and a cripple. And we have talent."

Scandals in the Environmental Protection Agency (EPA) resulted in wholesale resignations. Administrator Anne Burford resigned with a dozen of her aides after the EPA was accused of ignoring violations of favored chemical companies. Growing out of the EPA scandals were even more serious charges against Rita Lavelle, head of the toxic-waste cleanup division. Lavelle perjured herself before Congress in testifying about her dealings with companies accused of violating EPA waste regulations and was sentenced to six months in jail.

Accused and found guilty of violating the 1978 Ethics in Government Act were Lyn Nofziger and Michael Deaver. Nofziger served as Reagan's political adviser. He left the White House in 1982 to open a consulting business and began lobbying his former colleagues for a contract with the Wedtech Corporation soon afterwards. The ethics law prohibited such lobbying within a year of leaving such a top government job. Nofziger was sentenced to ninety days in jail and fined $30,000.

Michael Deaver, another presidential adviser and close friend of Ronald and Nancy Reagan, was given a suspended three-year jail sentence and fined $100,000 in September of 1988 for lying about lobbying for big companies and foreign governments too soon after leaving the White House. An alcoholic, Deaver was told by U.S. District Judge Thomas Jackson that his battle with alcoholism "does not excuse, but it helps to explain" possible judgment lapses.

Deaver, like Nofziger, appealed his case on the grounds that the use of independent counsels selected under the ethics act might be unconstitutional. On June 27, 1989, Nofziger's conviction was overturned in a 2-to-1 ruling by a federal appeals court.

And so the misdeeds of Reagan aide after Reagan aide continued until, as presidential historian Shelley Ross has pointed out in the book *Fall From Grace*, "The sheer number of scandals in the Reagan Administration is unprecedented in American history." Up to a point President Reagan himself never seemed to be involved in any of his aides' peccadilloes, and none of their malfeasance in or out of office seemed to rub off on him. He remained so popular that he and George Bush easily defeated the Democratic presidential and vice presidential nominee, Walter Mondale and Geraldine Ferraro, in the national election in the fall of 1984.

Then the Iran-Contra scandal came to light in the autumn of 1986, and for the first time the credibility of the president himself began to be seriously questioned.

In one particular way the Iran-Contra scandal closely resembled the Watergate affair. This was in the disregard of the U.S. Constitution by the president and his principal aides who were involved. In both scandals the principal figures acted as if they were laws unto themselves or could take the nation's laws into their own hands and bend them to their will. At one point Oliver North, a key figure in the Iran-Contra affair, stated flatly that he believed "the President has the authority to do what he wants to do with his own staff." These fascistic words echoed earlier similar words by the beleaguered Nixon: "When the President does it, that means it is not illegal."

Both North's and Nixon's totalitarian statements were clearly expressions of warped concepts of the American form of democratic government.

During the months following the release of the fifty-two American hostages in Teheran, a number of other Americans, as well as other foreign nationals, had been taken and held hostage in the Middle East. While several of these American hostages had been captured and held for one form of ranson or another in Beirut, Lebanon, it was widely accepted that the militants who had taken them hostage were Shiite Muslims fully backed if not sponsored by the Khomeini regime in Iran.

President Reagan and the U.S. State Department firmly denounced the Iranians as terrorists for persisting in taking these hostages. Reagan also called on all of the countries who were allies of the United States to join with America in an arms embargo on Iran and to make no concessions to the Iranian terrorists. Such an arms embargo, it was thought, would be especially harmful to Iran because it was engaged in a drawn-out war with its neighbor, Iraq.

In 1986 two of the hostages, the Reverend Benjamin Weir and Lawrence Martin Jenco, were freed. Then in November of 1986 it was suddenly announced that another American hostage, David Jacobsen, was being released by the Iran-backed Muslims. Jacobsen's release was widely heralded in the press as an apparent shift in Iranian policy. Up to this time the Iranians had demanded that certain Muslims held captive by Israel be released in exchange for the American hostages.

But on November 3 an article in a Lebanese weekly magazine, *Al Shiraa*, broke a story that indicated that it was apparently the United States that had secretly shifted its policy about dealing with terrorists. The story, given to the *Al Shiraa* editor, Hassan Sabra, by two high-level Iranian secret agents, stated that Robert McFarlane, former national security adviser to President Reagan, had visited Teheran as a White House envoy. The purpose of McFarlane's mission, according to the story, was to arrange with the Ayatollah Khomeini regime a shipment of U.S. weapons in exchange for the seven Americans then held hostage in the Middle East.

On the very same weekend that this story appeared in *Al Shiraa*, hostage Jacobsen was flown out of Beirut to Cyprus and then to the United States. Foreign correspondents in Beirut at first paid little attention to the story in *Al Shiraa* until an Islamic militant organization announced that Jacobsen had been released only after certain overtures had been made by the White House.

Once the story reached the United States, reporters began asking questions about McFarlane's trip to Teheran. White House press secretary Larry Speakes stated flatly that he knew nothing about such a story. McFarlane said the report was "fanciful, largely fictitious." The U.S. State Department denied it. But the arms-for-hostages rumors kept pouring in, and on November 6 two U.S. newspapers, the *Washington Post* and the *Los Angeles Times*, broke major stories reporting that secret arms-for-hostages deals between the United States and Iran had been going on for some months.

There was an immediate outcry from Congress, where a complete investigation was demanded. The American public also clamored for an explanation since it remembered only too well the daily television broadcasts of the hostages being held in Teheran during the Carter administration when the Iranians had been shown burning U.S. figures in effigy as well as burning the American flag and otherwise insulting the United States. People simply could not believe that Ronald Reagan, the president who had been so outspoken against the Iranians and other terrorists, had suddenly and secretly broken his word and tried to work out a deal with the despised Khomeini regime.

President Reagan and his aides were at first inclined, just as were Nixon and his aides in the Watergate affair, to "stonewall" it—that is, insist that nothing of much importance had happened and whatever had happened did not involve the White House. Stonewalling, however, proved to be impossible as public clamor for an explanation mounted and as letters and telegrams of protest poured into Congress and the White House. Finally, on Thursday night, November 13, President Reagan delivered a televised statement from the Oval Office about the Iran affair.

"The charge has been made," the president said, "that the United States has shipped weapons to Iran as ransom payment for the release of American hostages in Lebanon; that the United States undercut its allies and secretly violated American policy against trafficking with terrorists.

"Those charges are utterly false. The United States has not made concessions to those who hold our people captive in Lebanon, and we will not. The United States has not swapped American weapons for the return of American hostages, and we will not."

The president was, of course, mistaken. The United States had been doing exactly what he denied it was doing for many months. Actually, according to public opinion polls, not much of the public believed the president's denials, and a week later he admitted there had been a secret arms deal in which a third country was involved. The "third country" was Israel. Some time after that statement President Reagan said he had not approved the arms deal. But then he backed off behind the declaration, "I don't remember—period."

The only time Reagan ever came out and flatly admitted an

arms-for-hostages operation had been undertaken by the United States was in a speech on March 4, 1987, in which he confessed, "What began as a strategic opening to Iran deteriorated in its implementation into trading arms for hostages. It was a mistake."

But even though the president said these words—written for him by speechwriter Landon Parvin—he quite obviously never personally fully believed that he and his aides had traded arms for hostages or dealt with the Ayatollah Khomeini. Even when congressional investigators showed Reagan a document he himself had signed approving a shipment of antiaircraft missiles to Iran, Reagan read it and, smiling triumphantly, declared. "It doesn't say arms are being swapped for hostages." This incident was later reported in Jane Mayer and Doyle McManus's book *Landslide*, which is a detailed account of the Iran-Contra affair.

As Mayer and McManus also report, the arms-for-hostages deal began in the summer of 1985, when the name of a Middle East arms merchant, Manuchar Ghorbanifar, was presented to National Security Adviser Robert McFarlane in Washington. (McFarlane did not resign as national security adviser until late that year. He would be replaced by McFarlane's deputy, Navy Vice Admiral John M. Poindexter.)

Ghorbanifar was suggested to McFarlane by an Israeli agent, David Kimche, as a man the United States might be able to deal with in getting American hostages released. The release of one specific hostage, William Buckley, was especially sought by the United States because Buckley was a captured CIA agent who, it had been reported, was being tortured by the Shiite Muslims to obtain information about secret American operations. Ghorbanifar, Kimche told McFarlane, had contacts with moderate Iranian leaders who weren't directly associated with the wild-eyed radicals immediately surrounding Khomeini.

Shortly after McFarlane's talk with Kimche, one of McFarlane's aides, Marine Lieutenant Colonel Oliver North, who had served for five years on the National Security Council, reported to coworkers that he learned that Israel had been engaged in trading arms to Iran for Jewish refugees for several years. If this method worked for obtaining Jewish refugees, Colonel North asked, why shouldn't it work for obtaining American hostages?

McFarlane and several other NSC members as well as CIA chief William Casey and several of his staff agreed with North. But would the president and his aides go along with dealing with Iran, even indirectly? It turned out that Secretary of Defense Caspar Weinberger and Secretary of State George Shultz opposed such a deal, even through a third party, but apparently President Reagan and several other aides favored it. McFarlane later said President Reagan had, in fact, heartily approved such a deal. No written record, however, was made of such an approval. Later Reagan could not recall any such discussion with McFarlane, so it is not clear whether Reagan ever gave explicit approval.

Nevertheless, the deal proceeded, and a number of both antitank and antiaircraft missiles were shipped to Iran via Israel. But no hostages were immediately forthcoming. Finally, however, on September 15, 1985, one hostage was released. But it was not William Buckley, the CIA agent. Instead it was the Reverend Benjamin Weir. Weir reported that Buckley had been dead for several months and that the six other American hostages would also be killed unless the United States pressured Israel to release a number of Kuwaitee prisoners it held.

Perhaps because of disappointment over not getting back all of the hostages, the United States began to engage in negotiations more directly with Iran in 1986. But by now another key element had entered the picture.

This additional facet had to do with obtaining funds from the Iranian arms deals to support rebel forces in the Central American country of Nicaragua who were trying to overthrow the Nicaraguan government. Since coming into office in 1981, President Reagan and his administration had opposed the authorized government of Nicaragua, claiming it was Communist and supported by the Soviet

Union. Members of the authorized government were known as the Sandinistas. The rebel forces were called the Contras. Reagan had done everything in his power to support the Contras despite much opposition from the American public and the U.S. Congress.

Congress had blown hot and cold in its support of the Reagan administration's pro-Contra stance. For a time it funded the Contras with money for both arms and non-military supplies. Then, responding to the noninterventionist attitude of the American public, Congress stopped military aid. Then it stopped all aid and even passed the Boland Amendment, named after Congressman Edward P. Boland of Massachusetts, that halted all funding for the Contras.

Despite the Boland Amendment, American aid to the Contras continued. The operation was handled covertly through the CIA and aides of the president. They solicited large sums of money from countries that were allies of the United States and then turned these funds over to the Contras. Now with the arms-for-hostages deal with Iran in the works, several people saw a golden opportunity to obtain additional money for the contras by selling some of the arms and using the profits for the Contra cause. The question of illegality or unconstitutionality apparently did not cross the minds of these opportunists.

Oliver North was perhaps the key opportunist in this situation. He was aided and abetted by his new boss, Vice Admiral John Poindexter, who had succeeded McFarlane as national security adviser. In later testimony before a congressional committee, Ollie North was not certain who had come up with the idea of selling arms to fund the Contras—perhaps, he thought, it was Ghorbanifar—but North had immediately considered the idea "neat."

To aid him in his covert arms operation, which was called "Project Democracy" or "Operation Democracy," North enlisted the aid of retired Air Force General Richard V. Secord and Iranian-born but now American citizen Albert Hakim. Secord and Hakim had worked together before on secret arms deals, and both had also worked with Ghorbanifar. Secord came highly recommended by the CIA's Casey.

In all of his later testimony, North insisted he was in on the arms deals for purely idealistic and patriotic motives. Secord and Hakim in their congressional testimony left little doubt that idealism was a secondary motive while personal monetary profit ranked number one.

During the first several months of 1986, several shipments of arms were made to Iran. No additional hostages, however, were forthcoming. In an attempt to break this hostage deadlock, it was decided that Ollie North and former security chief McFarlane would personally fly to Iran and consult with Iranian leaders. Bearing false passports and carrying poison pills with which they could commit suicide if their mission went wrong, the two American emissaries flew to Teheran in an unmarked Israeli plane at the end of May.

Actually their trip accomplished nothing. A fourth load of military material was delivered as a result of this mission, but again no more hostages were released. Upon returning home, McFarlane reported on the mission's failure directly to the president. According to McFarlane, the president encouraged McFarlane, North, and Poindexter to continue their efforts through Operation Democracy.

Finally, some weeks later, a third American hostage was released. This was Lawrence Martin Jenco, who turned up free in Damascus. Whether or not Jenco's release had anything to do with Operation Democracy was not clear, although North and Ghorbanifar were conferring in Frankfurt, Germany, at the time and Ghorbanifar told North Jenco's release had been arranged in exchange for a promise of more antiaircraft missiles and parts from the United States. North arranged for the delivery of this material.

Despite their best efforts to conceal the activities of Operation Democracy, rumors of its activities began to appear in the American press. Then, in the fall of 1986, some leaflets appeared in Teheran reporting on McFarlane and North's mission to confer with Iranian officials the previous spring. These leaflets were forwarded to the United States, where reporters immediately began to query the White House about the McFarlane-North mission. White House spokesmen were still denying everything when David Jacobsen was released on Sunday morning November 2, and the next day the magazine *Al Shiraa* in Beirut broke its story about the secret U.S. dealings with Iran.

What eventually followed after the revelation and final admission by the Reagan administration that it had indeed been dealing with the Iranian government were several federal investigations. The first was by a three-man commission headed by former Senator John Tower of Texas, who had also been chairman of the Senate Armed Services Committee. The other two members were Brent Scowcroft, who had been President Ford's national security adviser, and former Maine senator and presidential aspirant Edmund S. Muskie. Muskie had also been President Carter's secretary of state. This blue-ribbon committee, which first met on December 1, 1986, was officially named by President Reagan, and predictions were that it would result in a whitewash of the administration. Predictions were wrong. When it reported its findings, it came down hard not only on President Reagan but also on the members of the National Security Council and others who had been engaged in Operation Democracy.

The Tower Committee report, delivered on February 26, 1987, said the president was a "hands-off" manager who delegated too much responsibility to subordinates and retained too little interest in important details and developments. The report also made the following assertions: "Confused and unaware, Reagan had allowed himself to be misled by dishonest aides and staff members. Robert McFarlane had failed to keep the Cabinet informed of the matter, and Vice Admiral John M. Poindexter, McFarlane's successor as National Security Adviser, had actively misled members of the Cabinet."

In response to these and other accusations, President Reagan said, "I did not know about the diversion of funds. Indeed I did not know there were excess funds." Also in reaction to the committee's findings, the president fired both Admiral Poindexter and his NSC aide Oliver North. Frank Carlucci, a career intelligence officer, became the new head of the National Security Council.

116

A second federal Iran-Contra investigation was conducted by a joint Senate and House of Representatives committee headed by Senator Daniel K. Inouye of Hawaii and Representative Lee H. Hamilton of Indiana. A third federal investigation was conducted by an independent counsel or prosecutor, Lawrence E. Walsh.

The Tower investigation had been conducted in private. Most of the joint congressional Iran-Contra committee hearings were not only public but also televised and provided an atmosphere reminiscent of the Watergate hearings during the Nixon administration. And, as in the case of Watergate, those witnesses who televised best, who created the most charisma or physical attractiveness on TV, became the most popular with the viewing public.

The undoubted star of the televised Iran-Contra hearings was Lieutenant Colonel Oliver North. Resplendent in his Marine Corps uniform, his left chest covered with service ribbons, Colonel North seemed to be the embodiment of the patriotic all-American military hero. President Reagan had already referred to North as a hero, despite the fact that he was fired for his duplicity, and North's boyish charm and evident sincerity seemed to radiate from the TV screen as he testified that his efforts were all made out of sheer patriotic zeal.

North's secretary, Fawn Hall, also proved to be a remarkably charismatic witness. She too seemed to have as little respect for the law as her boss, admitting to smuggling key documents regarding the NSC's role in the Iran-Contra affair out of North's office in order to conceal the information from the investigators. She also aided North in destroying pertinent documents by shredding them. Some of this shredding took place at the very time that Attorney General Meese's investigators were examining NSC material in North's office. Fawn Hall's atittude was perhaps best expressed in her statement, "Sometimes you have to go above the written law, I believe."

Both North and his boss, Admiral Poindexter, especially the latter, made it clear in their testimony that they believed they knew what the president wanted accomplished as far as freeing the hostages and supporting the Contras were concerned and that, therefore, it wasn't necessary to consult with the president on all of their covert activities. Poindexter, in fact, made a point of protecting the president from such knowledge so that no one would be later able to accuse the president of breaking any moral or other laws. This assumption that they knew not only what was best for the country in general but also for the president in particular caused Congressman Lee Hamilton to state bluntly:

As I understand your testimony, you did what you did because . . . you believed it was for a good cause. I cannot agree that the ends . . . justified these means—that the threat in Central America was so great that we had to do something, even if it meant disregarding constitutional processes, deceiving the Congress and the American people. The means employed were a profound threat to the democratic process . . . . Methods and means are what this country is all about. We subvert our democratic process to bring about a desired end—no matter how strongly we believe in that end—we've weakened our country, and we have not strengthened it. A few do not know what is better for Americans than Americans know for themselves. If I understand our government correctly, no small group of people, no matter how well-intentioned they may be, should be trusted to determine policy.

Senator Inouye added:

Speaking for myself I see it as a chilling story, a story of deceit and duplicity and the arrogant disregard of the rule of law. It is a story of withholding vital information from the American people, from the Congress, from the Secretary of State, from the Secretary of Defense, and according to Admiral Poindexter, from the President himself.

The congressional Iran-Contra hearings lasted for three months during the summer of 1987. When they were over, a report was issued that severely criticized President Reagan for allowing his administration to make a foreign policy error of major proportions. The president, however, did not appear to have violated any criminal statute and thus was not liable to impeachment. There was no solid evidence that President Reagan knew about the diversion of profits from the arms sales to the Contras. Such knowledge, according to Hamilton, would have made Reagan guilty of an impeachable act. But Poindexter and North had kept this knowledge from Reagan, using as an excuse the fact that they knew what the president wanted done but there was no need for him to know that it was being done.

NSC staff members were "out of control" according to the report, with Oliver North and Poindexter "privatizing" foreign policy and allowing Secord and his business partner Hakim to handle American negotiations with Iran and to control huge sums of money from the arms transactions. Such handling resulted in much of the money ending up in secret bank accounts in Switzerland.

When the arms flow to Iran did not result in the release of all the hostages, the arms flow continued, according to the report, because North and others believed the arms sales profits could provide a continuing source of money for the Nicaraguan Contras.

On Wednesday, March 16, 1988, the efforts of the independent counsel, Lawrence Walsh, resulted in several grand jury indictments being handed down in Washington, D.C. In these indictments Oliver North, John Poindexter, Richard Secord, and Albert Hakim were charged with conspiracy to defraud the United States, theft of government property, and other crimes. The four defendants pleaded not guilty.

Robert McFarlane, who had publicly confessed his own failings and tried unsuccessfully to commit suicide by taking an overdose of Valium, pleaded guilty, also in March of 1988, to four counts of withholding information from Congress. This reduced charge, merely a misdemeanor, was allowed when McFarlane agreed to testify against Oliver North.

CIA Director William Casey could not be charged with anything because he had died of brain cancer on the eve of the Iran-Contra hearings.

No sooner were indictments handed down on the Iran-Contra figures when there began to be much talk of the possibility of President Reagan's pardoning the four accused. But President Reagan denied he planned doing this, insisting that the law should run its course. Otherwise, he said, a pall of guilt would hang over the accused for the rest of their lives.

But the Reagan administration did go along with a not-so-subtle ploy on the part of Oliver North, who was to be the first of the accused to be tried. Through his legal counsel North requested that the government turn over to the court thousands of classified secret documents that North claimed were necessary for his trial. The administration refused, saying such disclosure would imperil national security.

Finally, an impatient Judge Gerhard A. Gesell placed a limit on the number of documents North could possibly need for an adequate defense and told North to pick out the documents he needed from among that number. North and his counsel were given until early in 1989 to make this selection, after which the trial was shortly to begin.

By the time the trial actually did begin in January, special prosecutor Walsh and his department of justice aides had spent more than two years and some $13 million preparing for it. At the last minute Walsh asked Judge Gesell to dismiss two of the more serious charges against North. These charges had to do with conspiracy against the government and theft of government property. Gesell said he was willing to dismiss these charges to avoid any further debate over the use of classified information.

North was then tried on what amounted to twelve lesser charges ranging from obstruction of Congress to the illegal destruction of government documents. The trial lasted until early May. When the verdict was handed down, both sides claimed victory. The jury found North not guilty of nine felony charges but convicted him on three other counts. The three charges of which he was found guilty were aiding and abetting an obstruction of Congress, destroying National Security Council documents, and receiving an illegal gratuity. The latter count was for a $13,800 home security system that North had accepted from Richard Secord.

Post trial interviews with the jurors made it clear some of them thought that North had been made the "fall guy" in the Iran-Contra affair, that he had merely been taking orders from several of his superiors. President Reagan, Vice President Bush, Admiral Poindexter, and perhaps others should have been on trial rather than North—or so some of the jurors apparently thought.

Admiral Poindexter and General Secord were scheduled to go on trial in 1990. Secord, however, avoided trial by pleading guilty to one count of lying to congressional investigators. In return, all other criminal charges were dropped. But Secord also agreed to cooperate and testify in any and all future Iran-Contra trials. This meant he would testify in the forthcoming trial of former National Security Adviser Admiral Poindexter. There were indications also that Albert Hakim would enter into a similar plea-bargaining agreement.

North was given a three-year suspended jail term, a $150,000 fine, and placed on probation for two years. In addition, he was ordered to perform 1200 hours of community service with a model antidrug program for youths from the District of Columbia. Finally, he was barred from ever again holding federal office. But his lawyer, Brendan Sullivan, said he would appeal the case. The first appeal was filed in late November 1989. Such appeals could cause the case and others following it to drag through the courts for years.

Further Reading

Bernstein, Carl, and Bob Woodward. *All the President's Men*. New York: Simon and Schuster, 1974 (Touchstone, paper, 1987).

Bradlee, Jr., Ben. *Guts and Glory—The Rise and Fall of Oliver North*. New York: Donald L. Fine, 1988.

Cockburn, Leslie. *Out of Control*. New York: Atlantic Monthly Press, 1987.

Cohen, William S., and George J. Mitchell. *Men of Zeal—A Candid Inside Story of the Iran-Contra Hearings*. New York: Viking, 1988.

Fox, Mary Virginia. *Mister President: The Story of Ronald Reagan*. Hillside, NJ: Enslow Publishers, 1986.

Grant, U.S. *Personal Memoirs*. Edited by E.B. Long. Cleveland and New York: World Publishing Co., 1952.

Keegan, John. "The Mask of Command." Chapter 3 in *Grant and Unheroic Leadership*. New York: Viking, 1987.

Lawson, Don. *A Picture Life of Ronald Reagan*. New York: Franklin Watts, 1985.

Manchester, William. *The Glory and the Dream*. New York: Bantam Books, 1975 (P).

Mayer, Jane, and Doyle McManus. *Landslide—The Unmaking of the President, 1984-1988.* Boston: Houghton Mifflin, 1988.

Morison, Samuel Eliot. *The Oxford History of the American People.* New York: Oxford University Press, 1965.

Moyers, Bill. "The Secret Government . . . The Constitution in Crisis." Public Affairs Television, Transcript Journal Graphics (P). New York: Alvin H. Perlmutter, 1987.

Ross, Ishbell. *The General's Wife—The Life of Mrs. U. S. Grant.* New York: Dodd, Mead and Co., 1959.

Ross, Shelley. *Fall From Grace.* New York: Ballantine Books, 1988 (P).

Russell, Francis. *The Shadow of Blooming Grove—Warren G. Harding in His Times.* New York-Toronto: McGraw-Hill, 1968.

White, Theodore H. *Breach of Faith—The Fall of Richard Nixon.* New York: Atheneum, 1975.

Whitney, David C. *The American Presidents.* Garden City, New York: Doubleday & Co., 1967-1985.

Index

A

Agnew, Spiro, Vice President, 73
    bribery scandal of, 86
Ames, Oakes, Congressman, Crédit
    Mobilier scandal and, 27-28
Appomattox Courthouse, surrender of
    General Lee at, 20
assassination attempt, on Ronald
    Reagan, 105-106

B

Babcock, Orville, General, Whiskey
    Ring scandal and, 29
Belknap, William W., Secretary of
    War, Indian territory trading
    post bribery and, 30
Blaine, James G., Speaker of the
    House, Crédit Mobilier
    scandal and, 28
Boland Amendment, 114
bootleg liquor, 50
Boutwell, George S., Secretary of
    Treasury, 24
Bristow, Benjamin H., Secretary of
    Treasury, Whiskey Ring
    scandal and, 29
Brooks, James, Congressman, Crédit
    Mobilier scandal and, 27-28
Buckley, William, 112, 113
Buckner, Simon, General, 18
Butterfield, Alexander, Watergate
    testimony of, 84-85

C

Cambodian bombing, during Nixon's
    administration, 78
Carter, Jimmy, President, 101, 103
Casey, William, CIA Director, 119
Chambers, Whitaker, 66
Chapin, Dwight, 76
Chase, Salmon P., Chief Justice, 6
Checkers speech, of Richard M.
    Nixon, 67-68
Civil Service Act of 1872, 25
Civil War, Ulysses S. Grant and, 17-20
Colfax, Schuyler, Vice President,
    Crédit Mobilier scandal
    and, 28
Colson, Charles, 77

Committee to Re-elect the President
    (CREEP), 80
Coolidge, Calvin, Vice President, 49
Crédit Mobilier scandal, of Ulysses S.
    Grant, 26-28
CREEP (Committee to Re-elect the
    President), 80

D

Daugherty, Harry M., Attorney
    General, 50, 58
Dean, John, 77
    Watergate sentence of, 87
Deaver, Michael, lobbying conviction
    of, 108
Dirty Tricks operation, in Nixon
    administration, 80
Domino Theory, 71

E

Eagleton, Thomas F., Senator, 82
Ehrlichman, John, 76
    Watergate sentence of, 87
Eisenhower, Dwight D., 67
Ellsberg, Daniel, Pentagon Papers and,
    79-80
Environmental Protection Agency,
    scandal of, 107-108
Ervin, Sam, Senator, 84

F

Fall, Albert B., Secretary of the
    Interior, 50, 52
    as anticonservationist, 53
    bribery of, 55
    Teapot Dome scandal and, 52-56
Ferraro, Geraldine, 108
Fish, Hamilton, Secretary of State, 24
Fisk, James, Jr., 25
Forbes, Charles R., Veterans' Bureau
    investigation and, 51
Ford, Gerald R., 86, 89
Fort Donelson campaign, of Ulysses S.
    Grant, 17-18

G

Garfield, James A., Congressman,
    Crédit Mobilier scandal
    and, 28

Gesell, Gerhard A., Judge, 120
Ghorbanifar, Manuchar, 112
gold market speculation, Ulysses S.
    Grant and, 25
Gould, Jay, 25
Grant, Ulysses S., 15-33
    Andrew Johnson and, 5-6
    battle of Shiloh and, 19
    birth of, 15
    bravery under fire of, 17
    cabinet appointments of, 23-24
    children of, 16
    cigar habit of, 32
    Civil War and, 17-20
    Crédit Mobilier scandal of, 26-28
    death of, 32-33
    drinking problems of, 18-19
    first presidential campaign of, 21
    Fort Donelson campaign of, 17-18
    gold market speculation and, 25
    Indian territory trading post bribery
        and, 30
    marriage of, 16
    Mexican War and, 16
    name change of, 15
    peacetime activities of, 16-17
    retirement from presidency and
        swindling of, 31
    second presidential campaign of,
        28-29
    surrender of General Lee at
        Appomattox Courthouse to, 20
    Unconditional Surrender, 18
    Vicksburg campaign of, 18-19
    as war hero, 21
    war memoirs of, 32-33
    West Point appointment of, 15
    Whiskey Ring scandal of, 29
    Wilderness campaign of, 20
Greeley, Horace, 29

H
Hakim, Albert, 114-115, 121
Haldeman, H.R., Chief of Staff, 75-76
    Watergate sentence of, 87
Hall, Fawn, 117
Harding, Warren G., 39-58
    affair with Carrie Phillips of, 43-44,
        47
    affair with Nan Britton of, 43,
        45-46, 47-48
    ancestry of, 39-40
    birth of, 39
    cabinet appointments of, 49-50
    death of, 56-57
    Harry M. Daugherty as kingmaker
        of, 42
    marriage of, 40-41
    newspaper career of, 40-41
    nomination for President of, 44-46
    political career of, 42
    presidential campaign of, 46-47
    radio speech of, 47
    in Roaring Twenties, 50
    Teapot Dome scandal and, 52-56
    Veterans' Bureau investigation and,
        51
    Voyage of Understanding of, 51-52
Hayes, Rutherford B., 31
Hinckley, John W., 106
Hiss, Alger, 66
Humphrey, Hubert, 72
Hunt, E. Howard, of Plumbers' Unit,
    80

I
impeachment
    of Andrew Johnson, 6-7
    of Richard M. Nixon, 88-89
Indian territory trading post bribery,
    Ulysses S. Grant and, 30
Iran, hostage capturing by, 103
Iran-Contra scandal, 109-121
    aid for Nicaraguan contras in,
        114-115
    hostages for guns in, 109-110
    indictments in, 119
    Israel as go-between in, 113
    joint congressional hearings into,
        117-119
    Oliver North and, 112-113
    Oliver North's trip to Iran in, 115
    President Reagan's denial of,
        111-112
    Tower Committee report of, 116

J
Jenco, Lawrence Martin, 115
Johnson
    Andrew, 5-7
        impeachment of, 6-7
        reconstruction of South and, 6
        Ulysses S. Grant and, 5-6
    Lyndon B., 71-72
Johnston, A.S., General, 19

K

Kennedy
  John F., 69-70
  Robert, Senator, 72
Klein, Herbert, 76
Kleindienst, Richard G., Attorney
  General, 88
Krogh, Egil, of Plumbers' Unit, 80

L

Lee, Robert E., General, 20
Liddy, G. Gordon, of Plumbers' Unit,
  80
listening devices, in Oval Office of
  Richard M. Nixon, 85-86

M

Magruder, Jeb, 77
McCarthy, Joseph, Senator, 69
McCord, James, Jr., Watergate
  testimony of, 84
McFarlane, Robert, Iran-Contra scandal
  and, 110, 115, 119
McGovern, George S., 82
Meese, Edwin, Attorney General, 106
Mexican War, Ulysses S. Grant and, 16
Mitchell, John N., Attorney General, 75
  as head of CREEP, 80
  Watergate sentence of, 87
Mondale, Walter, 108

N

Nicaraguan contras, aid for, 113-114
Nixon, Richard M., 63-89
  Alger Hiss affair and, 66
  anti-Communist theme of, 65, 66-67
  birth of, 63
  bombing of Cambodia and, 78
  cabinet and staff members of, 75-78
  Checkers speech of, 67-68
  children of, 65
  college career of, 64
  as congressman, 65-66
  defeated for Governor of California,
    70
  Dirty Tricks operation of, 80
  early life of, 64
  end of Vietnam War and, 83
  illegal wiretaps (bugging) and, 78
  impeachment proceedings against,
    88-89
  marriage of, 65

  as nominee for Vice President, 67
  pardoning of, 89
  Pentagon Papers and, 79
  Plumbers' Unit of, 79-80
  as president, 75-89
  presidential campaign against
    Hubert Humphrey of, 72-73
  presidential campaign against John
    F. Kennedy of, 69-70
  re-election in 1972 of, 83
  resignation from presidency of, 89
  as senator, 66-67
  taped conversations of, 84-86
  television debates vs. Kennedy of,
    69
  as vice president, 68-69
  Watergate affair and, 81-89
  Watergate cover-up and, 82
  Watergate evidence against, 87-88
Nofziger, Lyn, lobbying conviction of,
  108
North, Oliver, 109
  aid for Nicaraguan contras and, 114
  Iran-Contra scandal and, 112-113
  joint congressional hearings into
    Iran-Contra scandal and, 117
  trial of, 120-121
  trip to Iran of, 115

O

Operation Democracy, 114-115

P

Parker, Ely S., Commissioner of Indian
  Affairs, 24
Pennsylvania Fiscal Agency, Crédit
  Mobilier scandal and, 26
Pentagon Papers, in Nixon
  administration, 79
Plumbers' Unit, in Nixon
  administration, 79-80
Poindexter, John M., Admiral,
  Iran-Contra scandal and,
  116, 117-118, 121

R

railway, transcontinental, Crédit
  Mobilier scandal and, 26-28
Rawlins, John A., Secretary of War, 23
Reagan, Ronald W., 95-121
  as actor, 97-98
  administration of, 105-121

assassination attempt on, 105-106
birth of, 95
as campaigner for Barry Goldwater,
       99-100
children of, 99
denial of arms-for-hostages deal by,
       111-112
divorce from Jane Wyman of, 99
early life of, 95-96
Environmental Protection Agency
       scandal under, 107-108
as Governor of California, 100-101
Iran-Contra scandal and, 109-121
lack of ethics in administration of,
       106-108
marriage to Nancy Davis of, 99
as President of Screen Actors Guild,
       98
presidential aspirations of, 101
presidential campaign and election
       of, 102-103
as radio sports announcer, 96-97
television career of, 99
reconstruction of South, Andrew
       Johnson and, 6
Roaring Twenties, 50
Rodino, Peter, Representative, 89

S
Sandinistas, Nicaraguan, 114
Secord, Richard V., Air Force General,
       114-115, 121
Senate Watergate Investigating
       Committee, 84
Sherman, William T., General, 19
Shiloh, battle of, 19
Shriver, R. Sargent, Jr., 82
Sirica, John J., Judge, 84
South, reconstruction of, Andrew
       Johnson and, 6
speakeasies, 50
spoils system, 24-25
Stanton, Edwin M., Secretary of War, 6

T
Teapot Dome scandal, 52-56
   Albert B. Fall and, 52-56
   Pan American Petroleum and
      Transport Company of California
      and, 55
   Sinclair Oil Company and, 54-55
Tenure of Office Act of 1867, 6-7

Thomas, Lorenzo, Secretary of War, 6
Tilden, Samuel J., 31
Tower, John, Senator, 116
Tower Committee report, of
       Iran-Contra scandal, 116

U
Union Pacific Railroad, Crédit
       Mobilier scandal and, 26-28

V
Veterans' Bureau investigation, Warren
       G. Harding and, 51
Vicksburg campaign, of Ulysses S.
       Grant, 18-19
Vietnam War
   early involvement in, 70-71
   negotiated settlement of, 83
   during Nixon's administration, 78

W
Wallace, George C., 73
Watergate affair, 81-89
   cover-up of, 82
   evidence against Nixon and, 87-88
   initial burglary in, 81
   media investigation of, 82
   Nixon's taped conversations and,
       84-86
   Senate investigation of, 84-86
Watt, James, Secretary of Interior, 107
Whiskey Ring scandal, of Ulysses S.
       Grant, 29
wiretaps, illegal (bugging), in Nixon
       administration, 78
Woods, Rose Mary, 77-78

Z
Ziegler, Ronald, 76